The Politics of Development

The Politics of Development

An Introduction to Global Issues

John L. Seitz

Basil Blackwell

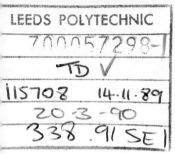
Copyright © John L. Seitz 1988

First published 1988

Basil Blackwell Inc.
432 Park Avenue South, Suite 1503
New York, NY 10016, USA

Basil Blackwell Ltd
108 Cowley Road, Oxford OX4 IJF, UK

Library of Congress Cataloging in Publication Data

Seitz, John L., 1931 –
    The politics of development.
    Includes Index.
    1. Economic develoment.   2. Developing Countries –
Economic policy.   3. Developing countries – Economic
conditions.   I. Title.
    HD82.8399 1987   338.9 87–20825
    ISBN 0–631–15746–8
    ISBN 0–631–15801–4 Pbk

British Library Cataloguing in Publication Data

Seitz, John L.
    The politics of development: an introduction
    to global issues.
    1. Economic development   2. Economic policy
    I. Title
    330.9   HD82
    ISBN 0–631–15746–8
    ISBN 0–631–15801–4 (pbk.)

Typeset in 11 on 13 pt Plantin
by Cambrian Typesetters
Printed in USA

To Leksi and Abigail
with hope for their future

Contents

Preface

In the 1950s and 1960s I went as an employee of the US government to Iran, Brazil, Liberia, and Pakistan to help them develop. Disillusionment came as I realized that we did not really know how to help these countries relieve their widespread poverty. And more disillusionment came when I looked at my own country and realized that it had many problems of its own which it had not solved. It was called "developed" but faced awesome problems which had accompanied its industrialization – urban sprawl and squalor, pollution, crime, materialism, and ugliness, among others. So, I asked myself, What is development? Is it good or bad? If there are good features in it, as many people in the world believe, how do you achieve them, and how do you control or prevent the harmful features? It was questions such as these which led me to a deeper study of development and to the writing of this book.

The book focuses on the role politics plays in solving certain key problems which have accompanied economic development in both the developed and less developed nations of the world.[1] Politics involves the efforts that are made to enable a people to live as a community. These efforts lead to the making of rules and decisions which are binding on all members of a society. Government is the only institution in modern societies which has the right to use physical force to make people obey its decisions. The rules and decisions which are made in politics usually deal with conflicts among groups within a society which want different things or disagree over how best to achieve goals generally desired by the society. While conflict is often a characteristic of politics, cooperation is also a feature of it as a society strives to achieve commonly desired goals. We will use this definition of politics in the book as we investigate how political systems are handling serious development problems connected with living standards, population growth, food production and consumption, energy use, the environment, and the use of technology.

"Development" as used in this book means economic growth plus the social changes caused by or accompanying that economic growth. In the 1950s and 1960s it was common to think of development only in economic terms. For many economists, political scientists, and government officials, development meant an increase in the per capita national income of a country or an increase in its gross national product (GNP), the total amount of goods and services produced. Development and economic development were considered to be synonymous. In the 1970s an awareness grew – in both the developing nations of the Third World[2] and the developed industrialized nations – that some of the social changes which were coming with economic growth were undesirable. More people were coming to understand that for economic development to result in happier human beings, attention would have to be paid to the effects that economic growth was having on social factors. Was an adequate number of satisfying and challenging jobs being created? Were adequate housing, health care, and education available? Were people living and working in a healthy and pleasant environment? Did people have enough nutritious food to eat? Every country is deficient in some of these factors and, thus, is in the process of developing.

In this book we will look at some of the most important current issues related to development. The well-being of people depends on how governments deal with these issues. It is not an exaggeration to say that the extinction of human life on this small planet has become a possibility because governments have not learned how to achieve adequate control of technology and its most dangerous product, nuclear weapons. Widespread poverty, the population explosion, food shortages, pollution, resource depletion, and energy shortages are all development issues. It is my hope that this book will aid the reader in understanding some of the major global issues today and the political choices that are connected to those issues.

The difficulty of making some of these political choices is illustrated by two case studies in the book. Arguments for and against certain choices connected with the issues of nuclear power and nuclear war will enable the reader to become immersed in the debates on these issues.

This book would not have been written if I had not received a grant from the Andrew W. Mellon Foundation. This grant, which was administered by Wofford College, allowed me to be excused from my teaching duties long enough to get the project well under way. Numerous colleagues have assisted me with their comments on parts of the manuscript. Especially useful were comments from Ab Abercrombie, Bud Talley, Crawford Young, and Tom Oleszczuk, who read all or most of the manuscript. Valuable secretarial services were provided by Mildred Thompson, Martha Mathews, and Joyce Blackwell. Jeanne Cheatham put most of the chapters on computer disks which greatly facilitated the preparation of the book. Denise Watson provided some research assistance.

Finally, male authors often end with a word of thanks to their wives for having typed the manuscript or kept the children quiet. Mine didn't do either. But my wife, Merike Tamm, gave me the idea for the course from which this book evolved. She was also an excellent editor and gave loving support while the work progressed. For this I thank her.

NOTES

1 The term "less developed" refers to a relatively poor nation in which agriculture or mineral resources are dominant in the economy while manufacturing and services play a minor role. About three-quarters of the world's people live in nations such as this, which are also called "developing." Since most of these nations are in the Southern Hemisphere, they are at times referred to as "the South." Industrialized nations, both capitalist and communist, are called "developed" nations. Most of them are located in the Northern Hemisphere so they are called "the North."

2 "Third World" refers to the poorer nations, or developing nations, of Latin America, Asia, and Africa. The "First World" is comprised of the capitalist industrial nations, while the "Second World" refers to the communist industrial nations. "Fourth World" is sometimes used to refer to that part of the Third World which is very poor and with little chance for becoming industrialized.

1

The Wealth and Poverty of Nations

The mere fact that opposing visions of economic development have grown to shape the international agenda is in one sense merely an indication that development concerns are receiving attention on a global scale for the first time in history.

Lynn Miller, *Global Order*

For most of history, human beings have been poor. Even today in some Third World countries the life expectancy of the average person is barely over 40 years, and malnutrition, illiteracy, and other deficiencies are common. A few individuals in many societies had a higher standard of living than their fellow humans, but the vast majority of people on earth shared a common condition of poverty.

The Industrial Revolution brought a fundamental change. New wealth was created in the industrializing nations in Europe and eventually came to be shared by larger numbers of people. And the difference between the rich and the poor in the world began to change. A few nations began to acquire higher living standards, and they began to pull away from the rest of the world which had not yet begun to industrialize. It is estimated that around 1850 the difference between the average incomes of people in industrializing Europe and those in non-industrial countries was 2 to 1. By 1950, the income gap between the rich and the poor countries was estimated to have grown to 10 to 1, and in 1960 it was 15 to 1. It is now predicted that, if present trends continue, the gap between the rich and poor nations could reach 30 to 1 by the end of the century.[1]

The growing gap between the rich and the poor is only one part of the picture of economic conditions world-wide. Another important development is the improvement in living standards for many, even in the poorer nations. While it is certainly true that the benefits of the impressive economic growth that has occurred in many developing nations since the end of World War II have been very unevenly shared – with many of the poorest receiving very little benefit, if any at all – it is also true that the lives of many others have improved. From 1960 to 1982 the average life expectancy of people in the developing countries rose from about 40 years to about 60 years, while the infant mortality rate dropped by around 50 percent and the primary school enrollment rate rose from about 50 to 95 percent.[2] But the hope that was fairly common in the 1960s of reducing the gap between the rich and the poor in the world had all but disappeared by the 1980s. The world continues to endure vast inequalities of wealth. About one-half of the world's people live in what are called low-income countries, with average gross national product (GNP) per person of about $250, while the Western capitalist countries in 1983 had an average GNP per capita of over $11,000.[3]

What makes some countries rich and some poor? There is no agreement on the answer to that question, but various views have been presented over the years. While vast differences among the nations of the world make generalizations hazardous, it can be useful to consider three of the most widely accepted approaches or views of economic development. The first approach – the orthodox or neoclassical approach – is adhered to by many in the capitalist countries.[4] Varieties of the second – the radical or exploitation approach – are commonly believed in communist countries and in large parts of the Third World. The third approach has roots in both preceding approaches and is called the growth-with-equity approach.[5]

THE ORTHODOX APPROACH

The orthodox approach holds that nations can acquire wealth by following four basic rules: first, the means of production – those things required to produce goods and services such as labor, natural resources, technology, and capital (buildings, machinery, and money which can be used to purchase these) – must be either controlled or owned by private individuals; second, there must exist markets in which the means of production and the goods and services produced are freely bought and sold; third, there must be capitalist firms which mold the means of production into goods and services; and fourth, there must be unrestricted trade at the local, national, and international levels.

Adam Smith, the founder of the orthodox approach, believed that the operations of labor were the key to increasing production. He argued that it was much more efficient that workers specialize in their work, focusing on one product rather than making many different products. If workers did this, and if they were brought together in one location so that their labor could be supervised, increased production would result. Smith also presented the idea that, if the owners of the means of production were allowed to freely sell their services or goods at the most advantageous price they could obtain, the largest amount of products and services would be produced and everyone would benefit. It is the prices in the markets which suggest to the businessman or businesswoman new profitable investment opportunities and more efficient production processes. Smith did not focus on the role of the entrepreneur, but later orthodox theorists did, making the entrepreneur – the one who brought the means of production together in a way to produce goods and services – a key component in this approach. Finally, Smith and other orthodox theorists emphasized the importance of free trade. If a nation concentrates on producing those products in which it has a comparative advantage over other nations, advantages which climate, natural resources, cheap labor, or technology give it, and if it trades with other nations which are also concentrating on those products that *they* have the greatest advantage in producing, then all will benefit.

The orthodox approach holds that government has a crucial but limited role in maintaining an environment in which economic activities can flourish. Government should confine its activities to: providing for domestic tranquility which would ensure that private property is protected; providing certain services, such as national defense, for which everyone should pay; enforcing private contracts; and helping to maintain a stable supply of money and credit.

The reason some nations are poor, according to the orthodox approach, is that they are deficient in one or more of the means of production, such as financial capital or an educated labor force, or that they do not follow the basic rules listed above.

Advocates of the orthodox approach point to the wealth of the USA and Western Europe as evidence of the correctness of their view. Even Karl Marx said that the 100 years of rule by capitalists were the most productive in the history of the world. And although an uneven distribution of income occurred in Western Europe during its early period of industrialization, the distribution of income later became much less uneven. This indicated that the new wealth was being shared by more and more people.

Nations such as Japan and West Germany, which came back from the devastation of World War II to create extremely strong economies by following the basic principles of the orthodox approach, are also cited as evidence of the approach's validity. Finally, some developing nations have achieved such impressive economic growth by following the principles of this approach that they have moved into a separate category of the Third World: the newly industrializing states. Many of these states, such as South Korea, Taiwan, Singapore, and the British colony Hong Kong, have achieved their high economic growth mainly by exporting light manufactured products to the developed nations.

Critics of the orthodox approach point to the high rates of unemployment that have existed at times in Western Europe and the USA. At the present time, high unemployment exists throughout the Third World, even in a number of nations that followed the orthodox approach and had impressive increases in their GNP. Much of the industry that has come to the Third World has been capital-intensive; that is, it uses large amounts of financial and physical capital but employs relatively few workers. Also, there is evidence that in countries such as Brazil, which has basically followed the orthodox approach for the past several decades, the distribution of income within the country became more unequal during the period the country was experiencing high rates of growth. The rich got a larger proportion of the total income produced in the country than before the growth began; and even worse than this is the evidence that the poor in countries such as Brazil probably became absolutely poorer during the period of high growth.[6] The economic growth which came to some developing nations following the orthodox approach failed to trickle down to the poor and, in fact, may have made their lives worse.

Critics of the orthodox approach have also pointed out that prices for goods and services set by a free market often do not reflect the true costs of producing those goods and services. Damage to the environment or to people's health which occurs in the production of a product is often a hidden cost which is not covered by the price of the product. Take for example a factory that pollutes the air while producing cars; the costs of cleaning soiled clothes and buildings and treating illnesses caused by damaged lungs are not borne by the factory owner or the purchaser of the car, but rather by the community as a whole.

THE RADICAL APPROACH

The radical approach has more to say about the causes of underdevelopment than it does about how development takes place. In a socialist country most of the means of production – land, resources, and capital – are publicly controlled to ensure that the profit which is obtained from the production of goods and services is plowed back to benefit the community as a whole. The prohibition on the private control or ownership of these so-called factors of production leads, according to the radical approach, to a relatively equal distribution of income, as everyone benefits from the economic activity, not just a few. The basic needs of all are provided for. The free market of the capitalist system is abolished and replaced with central planning. Prices are set by the central planners, and capital is invested in areas which are needed to benefit the society.

The root of the present international economic system where a few nations are rich and the majority of nations remain poor lies in the trade patterns developed in the sixteenth century by Western Europe.[7] ("Dependence theory" is the name given to this part of the radical approach.) First Spain and Portugal and then Great Britain, Holland, and France gained colonies – many of them in the Southern Hemisphere – to trade with. The imperialistic European nations in the Northern Hemisphere developed a trade pattern which one can still see clear signs of today. The mother countries in "the core" became the manufacturing and commercial centers, and their colonies in "the periphery" became the suppliers of food and minerals. Railroads were built in the colonies to connect the plantations and mines to the ports. This transportation system, along with the discouragement of local manufacturing which competed with that done in the mother countries, prevented the economic development of the colonies. The terms of trade – what one can obtain from one's export – favored the European nations, since the prices of the primary products produced in the colonies remained low while the prices of the manufactured products sent back to the colonies continually increased.

When most of the colonies gained their independence after World War II, this trade pattern continued. Many of the less developed countries still produce food and minerals for the world market and trade primarily with their former colonial masters. The world demand for the products from the poorer nations fluctuates greatly, and the prices of these products remain depressed. The political and social systems which developed in the former colonies also serve to keep the majority within these developing nations poor. A local elite, which grew up when these countries were under colonial domination, learned to benefit from the domination by the Western countries. In a sense, two societies were created in these countries: one, relatively modern and prosperous, revolved around the export sector, while the other consisted of the rest of the people who remained in the traditional system and were poor. The local elite, which became the governing elite upon independence, acquired a taste for Western products which the industrial nations were happy to sell them at a good price.

The present vehicle of this economic domination by the North of the South is the multinational corporation. Over 4,000 of these exist today, most with headquarters in the USA but a growing number of others headquartered in Europe and Japan. These corporations squeeze out small competing firms in the developing nations, evade local taxes through numerous devices, send large profits back to their headquarters, and create relatively few jobs, since the manufacturing firms they set up utilize the same capital-intensive technology that is common in the industrialized countries. Also, they advertise their products extensively, thus creating demands for things such as Coca Cola and color television sets while many people in the countries in which they operate still don't have enough to eat.

The advocates of the radical approach point to the adverse terms of trade which many developing nations face today. There is general agreement that there has been a long-term decline in the terms of trade for many agricultural and mineral products which the less developed nations export. There has also been great volatility in the prices of some of these products, with a change of 25 percent or more from one year to the next not uncommon for cocoa, rubber, sugar, copper, lead, and zinc.[8] Such fluctuations make economic planning by the developing nations very difficult. There is also clear evidence that the industrialized countries, while trading primarily among themselves, are highly dependent on the less developed countries for many crucial raw materials. These include chromium, manganese, cobalt, bauxite, tin, and of course oil.

Although international trade is still far from being the most important component of the US economy, it is a very important factor for many of the wealthiest corporations. In 1980 about one-half of the 500 wealthiest corporations listed in *Fortune* magazine obtained over 40 per cent of their profits from their foreign operations.[9] And some multinational corporations have financial resources larger than those of many Third World nations.

Finally, the defenders of the radical approach argue that there is little chance for many poor nations to achieve a fairer distribution of income as Europe did after it industrialized, because the controlling elites in underdeveloped nations today have repressive tools at their disposal (such as sophisticated police surveillance devices and powerful weapons) which the European elites did not have, and thus can deal with the pressures from the "have-nots" in a way the Europeans never could.

Critics of the radical approach point to the suppression of individual liberties in the Soviet Union, China, and other communist states as evidence that the socialist model for development has costs which many people do not like to pay. In fact, most revolutions have huge costs, leading to much suffering and economic deterioration before any improvement in conditions is seen; even after improvements do arrive, oppressive political and social controls are used by the leaders to maintain power. It is also likely that nations following this model to develop will substitute dependence on the Soviet Union, as Cuba has for example, for dependence on the West.

Central planning has proved to be an inefficient allocator of resources wherever it has been followed. Without prices from the free market to indicate the real costs of goods and services, the central planners can not make good decisions. And if efficient central planning has proved to be impossible in a developed country such as the Soviet Union, so also, but more so, has it proved to be a poor device in underdeveloped nations where governmental administrative capability is weak. A final negative feature of central planning is that it always leads to a large governmental bureaucracy.

Multinational corporations have produced jobs in the Third World which would not have existed without them; they have brought new technologies to the less developed nations, and have helped those nations' balance of payments problems by bringing in scarce capital and helping to develop export industries which earn much needed foreign exchange. These advantages are well known in the Third World, and explain why multinational corporations are welcomed by many less developed countries.

Political elites in developing nations have used the dependence theory, especially in Latin America where the theory is popular, to gain local political support among the bureaucracy, the military, and the masses. To blame the industrial nations for their poverty frees them from taking responsibility for their own development and excuses their lack of progress. It also frees them from having to clean their own houses of governmental corruption and incompetence, and to stop following misguided economic development approaches. The newly industrializing nations have shown that economic progress can be made even by developing nations that have a dense population and few, if any, natural resources – when orthodox principles are followed.

THE GROWTH-WITH-EQUITY APPROACH

The growth-with-equity approach borrows from and criticizes both the orthodox and the radical approaches. It criticizes the former for failing to improve the conditions of the poorest people; it also criticizes the socialist model for development, which is based on the radical approach, because growth-with-equity advocates believe it unlikely that many poor nations will have a revolution. Even if they did have one, there is no guarantee that the revolution would improve the conditions of the poorest. Also, history clearly shows that individual liberties are much restricted after modern revolutions.

Along with these criticisms of both the orthodox and the radical approaches comes some praise. The growth-with-equity approach adopts many of the capitalist institutions advocated by the orthodox approach since it believes these produce economic growth; it emphasizes egalitarian values which are important in the radical approach, since it believes these values assure that the growth will benefit those who need it the most.

The growth-with-equity approach is a fairly recent creation and contains a variety of components. The most common of these (presented below) are diverse – partly because of the belief that the individual differences among the poor nations call for different solutions to reduce their poverty. Nearly all those who advocate growth with equity share the belief that new efforts must be directed at the rural areas of the developing nations, where the majority still live and where the poor are concentrated. There is also agreement that more governmental action than the orthodox approach advocates is required if growth with equity is to be achieved. The free market cannot accomplish this on its own in most less developed countries.

1 *Expand employment.* The only way poverty will be eradicated in the Third World is if people have jobs. Development plans in Third World nations should shift from emphasizing the growth of the GNP to the creation of jobs. Many of the industrial methods which come from the West today utilize large amounts of physical capital but relatively few workers, creating a bad situation for the average developing nation adopting these methods, since it has little capital but many people looking for work. Appropriate or intermediate technology which utilizes many workers should be adopted by the poor nations instead of the high technology utilized in both the capitalist and socialist Western industrialized nations.

2 *Correct market distortions.* There are a number of distortions in

the markets of developing nations which favor the use of capital instead of labor. Governmental subsidies to capital exist; minimum wage legislation and extensive social welfare programs make the cost of labor higher to local industry than it should be, thus discouraging the use of labor; and governmental fiscal policies maintain artificially low interest rates.

3 *Shift capital investments.* Investments should be shifted away from large-scale, centralized projects which mainly benefit the high-technology industries and urban areas to projects which benefit the poor. Educational facilities, credit for rural farmers and industry, and public facilities for rural areas should be emphasized.

4 *Meet basic needs.* Food, safe water, clothing and shelter, medical services including family planning, education, and participation in decision-making should be provided to all. The emphasis on the development of human resources contained in this and the previous recommendation may lead to slower economic growth in the short run, but in the long run the increased productivity of the poor will benefit the whole society. It's a "trickle-up" strategy.

5 *Develop agriculture and rural areas.* Land reform must take the land away from the few large landowners, some of whom live in the cities, and turn it over to the people who actually farm the land. Aid should be given to increase agricultural productivity so that yields are greater but so is farm employment. The rural infrastructure such as roads, dams, schools, and irrigation systems should be improved, and small-scale rural industries should be promoted.

6 *Adopt a new international economic order.* The present international economic system was established after World War II when most of the Third World nations were still colonies. A major reorganization is now needed to help the poor nations of the world receive a fairer share of world wealth. The large fluctuations that occur in the prices of the commodities that many poor nations export need to be reduced; more international credit needs to be made available to the poor nations and some relief given on their huge debt. Rich nations need to lower their tariffs and remove their quotas on Third World exports, give more foreign aid, and give a larger role in the decision-making of key institutions such as the International Monetary Fund and the World Bank to the less developed nations.

Advocates of the growth-with-equity approach point to the examples of Sri Lanka, Taiwan, South Korea, and Costa Rica, which have basically followed this approach with good results. All of these countries had governments which encouraged capitalist institutions to operate, but also undertook efforts to make sure the benefits of the economic growth were widely shared. Revolutionary China and Cuba also followed growth-with-equity policies, but at the cost of extensive bureaucratization and the restriction of individual liberties.

The critics of the growth-with-equity approach can be divided between the traditionalists – the supporters of the orthodox approach – and the revolutionaries – the socialist supporters of the radical approach. The traditionalists state that the data are not adequate to show conclusively that the orthodox method has not benefited the majority in the poorer nations. Also, orthodox policies are being judged too soon, before they have had enough time to work. Some benefits have obviously trickled down to the poorest; for example, improved health conditions in the world can be seen in the lower infant mortality rates. The adoption of intermediate technology by developing nations means that they are not using the most modern techniques available and will probably never catch up to the industrial West. Slower economic growth will be achieved by those nations which follow some of the policies advocated by the growth-with-equity theory, such as the basic needs policy. Sri Lanka is pointed to with pride by the growth-with-equity advocates, but it remains a very poor country. And, finally, say the traditionalists, how do you prevent a welfare mentality from creeping in and undermining people's self-reliance when you adopt a basic needs policy?

The revolutionaries criticize the advocates of the new international economic order for believing that such a change would benefit the masses. They point out that many of the poorest people in the world live in South Asia in countries which participate in foreign trade very little. What is to prevent the leaders of the poorer nations from using the increased funds they obtain from such a new economic order from buying more military and police equipment to reinforce their own political control? Revolutionaries also ask why the advocates of growth with equity assume that Third World governments want to help their poor; it is more realistic to assume that the ruling elites in these countries are happy with conditions just as they are. Also, one should not assume that the middle class which exists in these countries would support a real growth-with-equity program since they want more things for themselves, such as a new car or a vacation in a foreign country. It is also naive to assume that land reform will take place in most Third World nations. Land reform changes the basic power structure of the society, and those in power will not permit such a reform to take place. Taiwan, South Korea, and Japan had land reform only after a war had weakened the position of those who controlled the land. Another reason Taiwan and South Korea are not good models for the Third World to follow is that these two countries have grown economically mainly by exporting goods to the USA. How many goods from Third World nations can or will the USA absorb?

CONCLUSIONS

The strength of the orthodox approach is that it appears to explain adequately some of the reasons why certain nations have become wealthy, but its weakness lies in failing to explain well why many nations have remained poor and how they can reduce their poverty. The radical approach, on the other hand, offers good insights into some of the many causes of world poverty, but is weak in explaining how wealth can be created. The growth-with-equity approach says something about both the wealth and poverty of nations and may, by adopting something from both the orthodox and the radical approaches while rejecting other parts, offer a way to improve the living conditions of the world's poorest.

Arthur Lewis, one of the leading experts today in development economics (the field of economics devoted to the study of the economies of the developing nations), identifies what has been learned so far about how to aid the poorest. There is general agreement today, he maintains, that the rural poor can be aided by a variety of governmental actions – such as land reform, agricultural extension services, educational and public health services – and technological improvements including irrigation, better varieties of seeds, and increased use of fertilizer.[10] This sounds very similar to the measures advocated by the growth-with-equity approach.

Lewis states there is less agreement among the experts on how to improve the conditions of the urban poor in the Third World. What is clear, according to him, is that the poorest nations since World War II have been those which had inadequate rainfall, making farming difficult, and those that had significant internal political turmoil, tending to discourage their own citizens as well as foreigners from making investments which would have led to new economic activity.[11]

The USA and Western Europe do not offer many relevant lessons for the poorest nations. Industrialization in the West took place under conditions vastly different from those now experienced by many poor nations. The Western nations were generally rich in natural resources in relation to their needs, or, if deficient, were able to get them from their colonies. Most developing nations today are not rich in the natural resources needed for industrialization (such as sources of energy), nor are they permitted to seize colonies. Also, they cannot adopt other means (now discredited) employed by the West during its early industrialization, such as child labor, 60-hour work-weeks, or subsistence wages for factory workers. In addition, the West, while experiencing an expansion of its population during its early development, did not come close to experiencing the vast population growth which is common today in many of the poorest nations. And Americans especially need to remember that the unique features their nation possesses – fertile land, rich natural resources, an abundance of fresh water in its numerous lakes and rivers, and a temperate climate – make their country atypical in the world. Americans used these gifts to create an unprecedented amount of material wealth – but with real costs, many of which will be examined in this book. The policies advocated by the orthodox approach generally worked well in America, where individual initiative was encouraged by a supportive government with limited powers.

Since much of the rest of the world does not share the assets Western Europe and the USA possess, what should they do to raise the living standards of the poorest? One might advocate revolution to break the repressive bonds common in a number of societies, but the suffering that revolutions cause and the uncertainty of their accomplishments make it difficult to recommend this course. But to counsel moderation and slow reforms also is difficult since, as historian Barrington Moore, Jr reminds us, it ignores the suffering of those who have not revolted. Moore believes that "the costs of moderation have been at least as atrocious as those of revolution, perhaps a great deal more."[12]

The poor nations should study carefully the experiences of Japan, South Korea, Hong Kong, Taiwan, and Singapore. These lands share with many of the poorest nations limited natural resources and large populations. A high regard for education and hard work in these Asian societies as well as stable governments have undoubtedly aided them. Government played a more active role in promoting economic activity in these places than that called for by the orthodox approach. It is unknown whether an export-based prosperity is a realistic possibility for many other Third World nations, or if such a prosperity will continue indefinitely for the Asian countries.

Where does this leave us? It should, I believe, leave us with a sense of humility if we are the rich, as we recognize how important factors outside of our personal control probably were in ensuring our richness. If we are the poor, it can leave us with an understanding of some of the causes of poverty and some suggestions of how nations might improve the lot of their poorest. And for both the rich and the poor, there should be an awareness that this is the first time in human history that there has been a global concern with issues of development – with why some are rich and many are poor. That we have not yet learned how to reduce the vast inequalities of wealth in the world should not be surprising. We may never learn how the South can catch up to the North. It seems likely now that within our lifetimes the gap between the rich and poor in the world will increase instead of decrease. But it is clear that we are learning, through trial and error, how to improve the lot of the poorest. Whether the poor and rich nations will have the political will – and ability – to do what is necessary to help the world's poor is not known.

The economies of many of the poor and rich nations are closely linked today. The rich industrial nations of the North need the resources and markets of the poor nations of the South, and the poor nations need to sell their products to the North.[13] And there is another way in which they are linked. Private banks and governments of the industrial countries and international agencies have

lent huge amounts of money to the less developed nations –
estimated to be $900 billion in the mid-1980s[14] – and the poorer
nations are having great difficulty paying the interest on these
loans. The interest payments of some Latin American nations are
now larger than the total funds they earn from their exports. If one
or more of the larger borrowers default on these loans, as some have
already come close to doing, it could set off an international
banking crisis. Poor and rich nations today are economically tied
together, and – as the following chapters on population, food,
energy, the environment, and technology will show – they are also
increasingly affected by a number of common global concerns.

NOTES

1 Lynn H. Miller, *Global Order: Values and Power in International
   Politics* (Boulder, Colo.: Westview Press, 1985), p. 129.
2 The World Bank, *World Development Report 1985* (New York:
   Oxford University Press, 1985), p. 1. While these figures leave one
   feeling encouraged, one must also be aware that much of the efforts of
   Third World governments to improve health services have been
   directed to the urban middle and upper classes rather than to the
   urban and rural poor. And the quality of education in the Third
   World may actually be worsening, since teachers' salaries have
   declined and the number of students per teacher has increased in
   many of the less developed nations. Thomas W. Merrick, "World
   Population in Transition," *Population Bulletin*, 41 (April 1986), p. 23.
3 World Bank, *World Development Report 1985*, pp. 174–5.
4 Current thinking among Western economists about economic development is considerably more complex than the simplified view of the
   orthodox approach presented below.
5 I am indebted to James Weaver and Kenneth Jameson, *Economic
   Development: Competing Paradigms* (Washington, DC: University
   Press of America, 1981), for much of the following material about the
   three approaches.
6 Irma Adelman and Cynthia Taft Morris, *Economic Growth and Social
   Equity in Developing Countries* (Stanford, Calif.: Stanford University
   Press, 1973), p. 189.
7 For a full discussion of the dependence theory see Bruce Russett and
   Harvey Starr, *World Politics: The Menu for Choice*, 2nd edn (New
   York: W. H. Freeman, 1985), ch. 16.

8 Ibid., p. 450.

9 Frederic S. Pearson and J. Martin Rochester, *International Relations: The Global Condition in the Late Twentieth Century* (New York: Random House, 1984), p. 383.

10 W. Arthur Lewis, "The State of Development Theory," *American Economic Review*, 74 (March 1984), p. 6.

11 Ibid., p. 5.

12 Barrington Moore, Jr, *Social Origins of Dictatorship and Democracy: Lord and Peasant in the Making of the Modern World* (Boston: Beacon Press, 1966), p. 505. Moore makes some harsh criticisms of revolutions also: "one of the most revolting features of revolutionary dictatorships has been their use of terror against little people who were as much victims of the old order as were the revolutionaries themselves, often more so" (p. 507).

13 In 1984 the USA absorbed about 60 percent of Third World manufacturers' exports, while the Third World took about one-third of US exports.

14 This estimate is by the World Bank, as reported in *The New York Times*, national edn, December 6, 1985, p. 34. For a full discussion of the debt issue see Henry L. Bretton, *International Relations in the Nuclear Age: One World, Difficult to Manage* (Albany, NY: State University of New York Press, 1986), pp. 232–7, and 290–6.

2

Population and Development

Prudent men should judge of future events by what has taken
place in the past, and what is taking place in the present.
Miguel de Cervantes (1547–1616),
Persiles and Sigismunda

THE CHANGING POPULATION OF THE WORLD

The population of the world is growing. No one will be startled by
that sentence, but what is startling is the rate of growth, and the
fact that the present growth of population is unprecedented in
human history. The best historical evidence we have today
indicates that there were about 5 million people in the world about
8000 BC. By AD 1 there were about 200 million, and by 1650 the
population had grown to about 500 million. The world reached its
first billion people about 1850; the second billion came about 1930.
The third billion was reached about 1960, the fourth about 1975,
and the fifth about 1987. These figures indicate how rapidly the
rate of population growth is increasing. Table 1 shows how long it
took the world to add each billion of its total population.

There is another way to look at population growth, one that helps
us understand the uniqueness of our situation and its awesome
possibilities for harm to life on this planet. Because children end up
having children of their own, the human population can – until
certain limits are reached – grow exponentially: 1 to 2; 2 to 4; 4 to 8;
8 to 16; 16 to 32; 32 to 64; 64 to 128; etc. When something grows
exponentially, there is hardly discernable growth in the early stages
and then the numbers shoot up. The French have a riddle which
they use to help teach the nature of exponential growth to their

Table 1 Time taken to add each billion of world population, 1850–1987

	Estimated world population (billions)	Years taken to add a billion to population
1850	1	2,000,000
1930	2	80
1960	3	30
1975	4	15
1987	5	12

schoolchildren. It goes like this: if you have a pond with one lily in it which doubles its size every day, and which will completely cover the pond in 30 days, on what day will the lily cover half the pond? The answer is the 29th day. What this riddle tells you is that if you wait until the lily covers half the pond before cutting it back, you will have only one day to do this – the 29th day – because it will cover the whole pond the next day.

If you plot on a graph anything that has an exponential growth, you get a J-curve. For a long time there isn't much growth, and then the bend of the curve in the "J" is reached and the growth becomes dramatic. Figure 1 shows what the earth's population growth curve looks like.

The growth of the earth's population has been compared to a long fuse on a bomb: once the fuse is lit, it sputters along for a long while and then suddenly the bomb explodes. This is what is meant by the phrases "population explosion" and "population bomb." The analogy is not a bad one. The world's population has passed the bend of the J-curve and is now rapidly expanding. The US government predicts that, if the present growth continues, the world's population will reach over 6 billion by the year 2000, shooting up from the estimated 4 billion in 1975, an increase of more than 50 percent in just 25 years. Table 2 gives population projections to the year 2000 for the world, major regions, and selected countries.

Table 2 shows that the largest growth in the future will be in the poorest countries of the world. The population of the more developed countries will grow by about 17 percent, while the

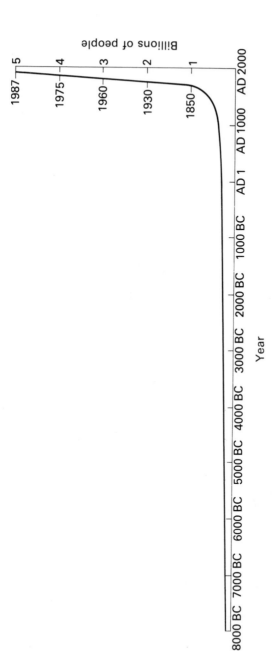

Figure 1 Population growth from 8000 BC to 1987

Table 2 Population projections for world, major regions, and selected countries

	Year 1975	Year 2000	% increase by 2000	Av. annual % increase	% of world population in 2000
	[millions]				
World	4,090	6,351	55	1.8	100
More developed regions	1,131	1,323	17	0.6	21
Less developed regions	2,959	5,028	70	2.1	79
Major regions					
Africa	399	814	104	2.9	13
Asia and Oceania	2,274	3,630	60	1.9	57
Latin America	325	637	96	2.7	10
USSR and Eastern Europe	384	460	20	0.7	7
North America, Western Europe, Japan, Australia, and New Zealand	708	809	14	0.5	13
Selected countries and regions					
People's Republic of China	935	1,329	42	1.4	21
India	618	1,021	65	2.0	16
Indonesia	135	226	68	2.1	4
Bangladesh	79	159	100	2.8	2
Pakistan	71	149	111	3.0	2
Philippines	43	73	71	2.1	1
Thailand	42	75	77	2.3	1
South Korea	37	57	55	1.7	1
Egypt	37	65	77	2.3	1
Nigeria	63	135	114	3.0	2
Brazil	109	226	108	2.9	4
Mexico	60	131	119	3.1	2
USA	214	248	16	0.6	4
USSR	254	309	21	0.8	5
Japan	112	133	19	0.7	2
Eastern Europe	130	152	17	0.6	2
Western Europe	344	378	10	0.4	6

Source: Council on Environmental Quality and the Department of State, *The Global 2000 Report to the President*, vol. 1 (Washington, DC: US Government Printing Office, 1980), p. 9.

population of the less developed countries will grow by about 70 percent. More than 90 percent of the growth of population from 1975 to 2000 will be in the poorer countries. An ever larger percentage of the world's population will be non-white and poor. High growth rates will take place in the less developed countries because a large percentage of their population consists of children under the age of 15 who will be growing older and having children themselves. If one plots the number of people in a country according to their ages, one can see clearly the difference between rapidly growing populations, which most less developed nations have, and relatively stable or slowly growing populations, which the more developed nations have. Figure 2 shows the difference between the populations of more and less developed nations of the world in 1975 and 2000. The age structure of the more developed countries is generally column-shaped, while that of the less developed countries is usually pyramid shaped. The USA, as a fairly typical more developed country, has a population distribution similar to the top figure, while Mexico, a fairly typical less developed country, has a population distribution similar to the bottom.

Another major change occurring in the world's population is the movement of people from rural to urban areas. While this is happening all around the world, the trend is especially dramatic in the Third World. People are fleeing the rural areas of the Third World to escape the extreme poverty which is common in those areas, and because the cities seem to offer a more stimulating life. Mostly it is the young people who go to the cities hoping to find work and better living conditions. But all too often jobs are not available in the cities either. These rural migrants usually settle in slums on the edges of the big cities. It is estimated that about one quarter of the population in many of the largest Third World cities live in such shanty towns (called "uncontrolled settlements" in government reports), and that they will contain about one-half of the population of these cities by the year 2000.[1] It is hard to imagine a city like Calcutta, India, getting any bigger. In 1950 it had a population of about 5 million, and hundreds of thousands of these people lived permanently on the streets; in the mid-1980s it had a population of about 11 million and nearly 1 million lived on the streets.[2] If the present rate of growth continues, it will have a

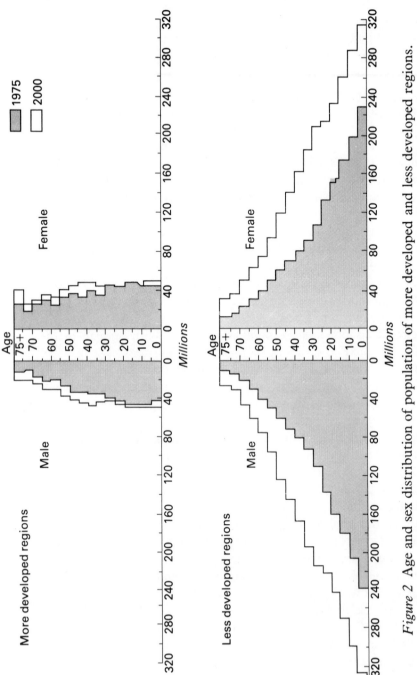

Figure 2 Age and sex distribution of population of more developed and less developed regions.

Source: Council on Environmental Quality and the Department of State, *The Global 2000 Report to the President*, vol. 1 (Washington, DC: US Government Printing Office, 1980), p. 11.

population of about 17 million by 2000. Table 3 gives the world's ten largest cities in 1950 and 1985 and the projected ten largest for the year 2000. Note that only two of the ten largest cities in the year 2000 – New York and Tokyo/Yokohama – are expected to be in the more developed countries.

CAUSES OF THE POPULATION EXPLOSION

While we have seen that the human population can grow exponentially, this fact alone does not explain why we are in a situation at present of rapidly expanding population. Exponential growth is only one of many factors which determine population size. Other factors influence how much time will pass before the doublings – which one finds in exponential growth – take place. Still other factors influence how long the exponential growth will continue and how it might be stopped. We will consider these last two matters later in the chapter, but will first look at some of the factors which drastically reduced the amount of time it took for the world's population to double in size.

The Agricultural Revolution, beginning about 8000 BC, was the first major event which gave population growth a boost. When humans learned how to domesticate plants and animals for food, they greatly increased their food supply. For the next 10,000 years until the Industrial Revolution, there was a gradually accelerating rate of population growth, but overall the rate of growth was still low because of high death rates, caused mainly by diseases and malnutrition. As the Industrial Revolution picked up momentum in the eighteenth and nineteenth centuries, population growth was given another boost as advances in industry, agriculture, and transportation improved the living conditions of the average person. Population was growing exponentially, but the periods between the doublings were still long because of continued high death rates. This situation changed drastically after 1945. Lester Brown of the Worldwatch Institute explains why that happened:

The burst of scientific innovation and economic activity that began during the forties substantially enhanced the earth's food-producing capacity and led to dramatic improvements in

Table 3 Ten largest cities in the world, 1950, 1985, and 2000

	1950 population (million)		1985 population (million)		2000 projected population (million)
1	New York, USA	12	Tokyo/Yokohama, Japan	19	Mexico City, Mexico	26
2	Shanghai, China	10	Mexico City, Mexico	17	São Paulo, Brazil	24
3	London, UK	10	São Paulo, Brazil	16	Tokyo/Yokohama, Japan	20
4	Tokyo/Yokohama, Japan	7	New York, USA	16	Calcutta, India	17
5	Beijing, China	7	Shanghai, China	12	Greater Bombay, India	16
6	Paris, France	6	Calcutta, India	11	New York, USA	16
7	Tianjin, China	5	Buenos Aires, Argentina	11	Shanghai, China	14
8	Buenos Aires, Argentina	5	Rio de Janeiro, Brazil	10	Seoul, South Korea	14
9	Chicago, USA	5	London, UK	10	Teheran, Iran	14
10	Moscow, USSR	5	Seoul, South Korea	10	Rio de Janeiro, Brazil	13

Source: UN Department of International Economic and Social Affairs, 1985.

disease control. The resulting marked reduction in death r₁ created an unprecedented imbalance between births a₁ deaths and an explosive rate of population growth. Thus, while world population increased at 2 to 5 percent *per century* during the first fifteen centuries of the Christian era, the rate in some countries today is between 3 and 4 percent *per year*, very close to the biological maximum.[3]

It was primarily a drastic reduction in the death rate around the world after World War II which gave the most recent boost to population growth. The spreading of public health measures, including the use of inoculations, to Third World countries enabled these countries to control diseases such as smallpox, tuberculosis, yellow fever, and cholera. Children and young adults are especially vulnerable to the infectious diseases; thus, the conquering of these diseases allowed more children to live and to bear children themselves.

While death rates around the world were dropping rapidly, birth rates remained generally high. Birth rates have been high throughout human history. If this had not been true, you and I might not be here today, since high birth rates were needed to replenish the many people who died at birth or at an early age. (If you walk through a very old cemetery in the USA or especially in Europe, you can see evidence of this fact for yourself as you pass the family plots with markers of the many children who died in infancy and in adolescence.) Birth rates remained high right up until the late 1960s, when a lowering of the rate world-wide was seen, which is probably the beginning of a gradual lowering of the birth rate around the world.

The birth rate today has dropped significantly in the developed nations but remains high in most Third World countries. There are a number of reasons for this. First, many poor people want to have many children. If many of them die in infancy, as they still do in countries such as India, Pakistan, Bangladesh, and in tropical Africa, many births are needed so that a few children survive. If the poor families are peasants, as many of them are, sons are needed to work in the fields and to do chores. And since there are rarely old age pension plans in Third World countries, at least one son (and preferably two) is needed to ensure that the parents have someone to take care of them when they are old and can no longer work. These needs are behind the common greeting to a woman in rural India: "May you have many sons."[4]

Poor families also want children to provide extra income to the family. Before child labor laws severely restricted their employment in factories in the USA and Europe, it was common for children to take paying jobs to help the family gain income. A study of an Indian village found that the poorest families had many children since they felt that increased numbers meant more security and a better chance for prosperity.[5]

Other reasons for continued high birth rates in poor countries are tradition and religion. Tradition is very important in most rural societies, and traditionally families have been large in rural settings and among poor people. One does not break with such a tradition easily. Also, religion is a powerful force in rural societies and some religions advocate large families. The Catholic religion is powerful in rural Latin America, especially with the women, and many obey the Catholic Church's prohibition against the use of contraceptives. In Mexico men have commonly regarded a large number of children as proof of their masculinity.

The unavailability of birth control devices is also often cited as a reason for the high birth rates in developing nations. No doubt this does have an effect, but population experts are now placing less emphasis on this reason than they did before. Although many children in poorer families are unplanned and unwanted, many others are wanted. People have generally throughout history found ways to have fewer children if they strongly want smaller families. The remarkable reduction of the birth rate in most European countries in the late nineteenth and early twentieth centuries was accomplished in spite of the fact that modern contraceptives were generally absent, especially in the Catholic countries.

POPULATION GROWTH AFFECTS DEVELOPMENT

How does population growth affect development? While there is no easy answer to the question of what is "too large" or "too small" a population for a country – a question we will return to in the final section of this chapter – we can identify some obvious negative features of a rapidly growing population, a situation which would apply to many Third World countries today.

Too Rapid

When you look at the age distribution of the population in Third World nations (figure 2), you notice that a large percentage of their people are below the age of 15. This means that these countries have a large portion of their population which is mainly non-productive. While children do produce some goods and services, as we have seen above, they consume more goods and services than they produce. Food, education, and health care must be provided to them before they become old enough to become productive themselves. Obviously, if a nation has a large portion of its population in the under-15 age group, its economy will be faced with a huge burden.

A rapidly growing population also puts a great strain on the resources of the country. If the population is too large or the growth too rapid, people's use of the country's resources to stay alive can actually prevent the biological natural resources from renewing themselves. This can lead to the land becoming less fertile, and the forests being destroyed. An example of this is the making of patties out of cow droppings and straw by women in India and Pakistan. These patties are allowed to dry in the sun and are then used for fuel. In fact, dung patties are the only fuel many peasants have for cooking their food. But the use of animal droppings for fuel prevents essential nutrients from returning to the soil, thus reducing the soil's ability to support vegetation.

A large population of young people also means that there will be a terrific demand for jobs when these children get old enough to join the labor force – jobs which are unlikely to exist. The ranks of the unemployed and underemployed will grow in many Third World nations, and this can easily lead to political and social unrest. As we saw earlier in this chapter, people from the rapidly growing rural areas of the Third World are heading for the cities hoping to find work. The scarcity of jobs is undoubtedly a contributing factor in the high rates of urban crime. An experience in Liberia helped me to understand this point. I lived at different times in both the capital city of that country and in a small village in the rural area.

Once while I was in Monrovia, the capital, a thief stole my wallet and watch from under my pillow, which was under my sleeping head at the time. Such an event was unheard of in the rural areas, but was not that uncommon in the city. After the theft happened, I was happy to return to my "primitive" village where I felt much safer.

Rapid population growth also has a harmful effect on the health of children and women. Malnutrition in infancy can lead to brain damage, and child-bearing frequently wears women down. This is what happens to many Third World women:

> After two decades of uninterrupted pregnancies and lactation women in their mid-thirties are haggard and emaciated, and appear to be in their fifties. As researchers Erik Eckholm and Kathleen Newland point out, such women are "Undernourished, often anemic, and generally weakened by the biological burdens of excessive reproduction," they "become increasingly vulnerable to death during childbirth or to simple infectious diseases at any time," and "their babies swell the infant mortality statistics."[6]

A rapidly growing population also puts a tremendous strain on the ability of a nation to provide housing for its people. The poor condition of much of the housing in the Third World is something that makes a lasting impression on foreign visitors to these countries – that is, if they leave the Hilton Hotels where they often stay. Overcrowding also is produced by an excessive and rapidly growing population, and that leads to a scarcity of privacy and to limited individual rights.

Not surprisingly, a study sponsored by the US National Academy of Sciences to explore the relationship between population growth and economic development concluded in the mid-1980s that slower population growth would aid economic development in most of the less developed nations.[7]

Too Slow

A country's population growth rate can also be too slow to support a high level of economic growth. Partly because of low birth rates, a number of European countries had to import unskilled workers during the 1950s and 1960s from Turkey, southern Italy, and other relatively poor areas of Europe and north Africa. Some business people get worried if the population stops expanding since they see a growing population as representing more consumers of their products. But a number of the industrial countries have shown in the post-World War II period that a high level of economic growth can be obtained even when population growth is low. Japan is a good example of such a country.

Age Distribution and the Problems it Creates

I have so far discussed problems which are created when a country has a large portion of its population aged 15 or less. But special problems are also created when the proportion of a population which is over 65 starts to expand. The USA in the early 1980s was faced with problems with its Social Security system which provides pensions to retired persons. As the percentage of the US population which is over 65 expands because of advances in health care, and the number of new workers is reduced because of low birth rates, the ratio of working-age people to retired people declines and puts strain on the pension system. (It is the payments from the current workers which provide money for the retirement benefits.) A congressional report in 1980 stated that there were 5 persons of working age for every person over 65, but that if present birth and death trends continue, this ratio could decline to 3 to 1 by the year 2030.[8] About 25 percent of the federal budget was going to programs to benefit the aged in 1980, and projections are that this could increase to over 30 percent by the year 2000 and to about 50 percent by the year 2020![9]

Is Population Growth the Cause of Poverty, or Is Poverty the Cause of Population Growth?

The first international conference on population was held in 1974 in Romania under the sponsorship of the United Nations. It was anticipated that this conference would dramatize the need for population control programs in the Third World, but instead, a debate took place between rich and poor countries over what was causing poverty: population growth or underdevelopment. The USA and other developed nations argued for the need for birth control measures in the poorer countries, while a number of the poorer countries argued that what was needed was more economic development in the Third World. Some Third World countries called for a new international economic order to help the Third World develop. They advocated more foreign aid from the richer countries, and more equitable trade and investment practices. The conference ended with what seemed to be an implicit compromise: that what was needed was both economic development and population control, and that an emphasis on only one and an ignoring of the other factor would not work to reduce poverty.

In 1984 in Mexico the UN held its second world population conference. The question of the relationship between economic growth and population growth was raised again. The USA, represented by the Reagan administration, argued that economic growth produced by the private enterprise system was the best way to reduce population growth. The USA did not share the sense of urgency which others felt at the conference concerning the need to reduce the world's increasing population. It announced that it was cutting off its aid to organizations that promote the use of abortion as a birth control technique. In its rejection of the idea that the world faced a global population crisis, as well as its advocacy economic growth as the main population control mechanism, the USA stood nearly alone. The conference endorsed the conclusion reached at the first conference ten years before, that both birth control measures and efforts to reduce poverty were needed to reduce the rapidly expanding population of the Third World.

DEVELOPMENT AFFECTS POPULATION GROWTH

How does development affect the growth rate of population? There is no easy answer to that question, but population experts strongly suspect that there *is* a relationship, since the West had a fairly rapid decline in its population growth rate after it industrialized. In the nineteenth century Europe began to go through what is called a "demographic transition."

Demographic Transition

A demographic transition has three basic stages. In the first stage, which is often characteristic of pre-industrial societies, there are high birth rates and high death rates which lead to a stable or slowly growing population. In the second stage, which most industrial nations passed through from about the mid-1800s to the mid-1900s, there is a rapid decline in the death rate as modern medicine and sanitation measures are adopted, which is followed, after some delay, by a drop in the birth rate. During this second stage of transition population increases rapidly, since the reduction in the death rate takes place before the lower birth rate. In the final, and third stage, both the death and birth rates are low, and, as in the first stage, there is a stable or slowly growing population.

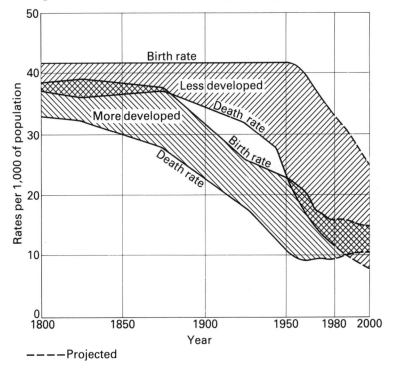

Figure 3 Demographic transition: more developed and less developed countries.

Source: "People" by Halfdan Mahler, *Scientific American* (September 1980), p. 75.

Figure 3 shows birth and death rates for both the more developed and less developed nations. The figure shows that the more developed nations are already in the third stage of the demographic transition but that the less developed nations are still in the second stage. It also shows some significant differences between the developed and developing nations' second stages. For the developed nations, the reduction in the death rate was gradual. The birth rate dropped sharply, but only after a delay which caused the population to expand. For the developing countries, the drop in the death rate has been sharper than it had been for the developed nations, and the reduction in the birth rate has lagged more than it had for the developed nations. Both of these facts have caused a much larger increase in the population of the less developed nations

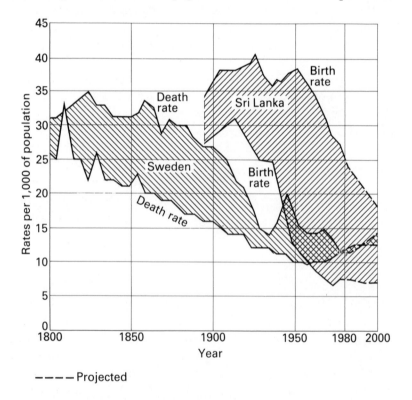

Figure 4 Demographic transition: Sweden and Sri Lanka.

Source: "People" by Halfdan Mahler, *Scientific American* (September 1980), p. 75.
Copyright © 1980 by Scientific American, Inc. All rights reserved.

than had occurred in the more developed nations. Figure 4 shows the population experiences of two countries: Sweden and Sri Lanka (formerly known as Ceylon). Sweden has passed through the demographic transition and has now reached zero population growth. Sri Lanka is experiencing a much more dramatic second stage than Sweden ever experienced and is having a much greater increase in population. Sri Lanka's population is still growing rapidly, and it does not have the opportunity to get rid of its excess population by sending it overseas to the USA, as Sweden had.

The differences in the experiences which Sweden and Sri Lanka are having, as well as the experiences of other developed and developing nations, have led many demographers to change the opinion they had in the 1950s that economic development would cause Third World nations to go through the same demographic transition – and thus achieve lower population growth – as the West had. There are obviously important differences between the Western experience and that of the Third World. Probably as important as the fact that death rates have dropped much faster in the Third World than they had for the West is the fact that the industrialization that is taking place in much of the Third World is not providing many jobs and is not benefiting the vast majority of people in those countries. A relatively small, modern sector *is* benefiting from this economic development, and the birth rate of this group is generally declining; but for the vast majority in the rural areas and the urban slums, the lack of jobs and continued poverty are important factors in their continued high birth rates.

Factors which Lower Birth Rates

If industrialization as it is occurring in the Third World is not an automatic contributor to lower birth rates, what factors do cause birth rates to decline? Certainly, better health care and better nutrition, both of which lower infant mortality and thus raise a family's expectations of how many children will survive, are important factors. (The irony here, of course, is that these advances, at least in the short run, tend to worsen the population problem since more children live to reproduce.) Another factor tending to lower birth rates is the changing role of women. The attainment of literacy by women is the social factor which appears

to correlate most closely with decreases in fertility.[10] Education for
women enables them to delay marriage, to learn about contraceptives, and to acquire different views of their role in society. And
their education allows them to obtain jobs which can often be of
more benefit to the family than having a larger family.

Actually, however, a little bit of modernization can be a bad
thing if one wants to reduce birth rates. In large parts of the Third
World women with a little exposure to Western ways are giving up
breast-feeding their babies and switching to bottle-feeding. Their
fertility goes up when they do this, since prolonged breast-feeding
naturally delays – sometimes for years – a woman's ability to
conceive again.

As Western nations industrialized, child labor laws, compulsory
education for children, and old age pension laws reduced the
economic incentives for having many children. When the West
industrialized, children changed from being producers on the farms
and in the early factories and became consumers and an economic
burden on a family. Also, as the West industrialized it became more
urban, and living space in urban societies is more scarce, and more
expensive, than in rural societies. The availability of goods and
services increases in urban societies, and families often decide to
increase their consumption of these rather than spend their income
on raising more children. Traditional religious beliefs, which often
support large families, also tend to decline in modern societies. All
of these factors lead many demographers now to believe that *both*
economic development, which benefits the many and not just the
few, and birth control measures are needed if the Third World is to
check its excessive population growth.

GOVERNMENTAL POPULATION POLICIES

Controlling Growth

Many governments today have some policies which try to control
the growth of their populations, but this is a very recent trend.
Traditionally, governments have sought to increase their
populations, either through the encouraging of immigration (as the
USA did in its early years) or through tax and other economic

assistance to those families with many children. As late as the mid-1970s, many governments had no population control programs. A survey of developing nations taken in conjunction with the 1974 UN population conference found that, out of 110 developing countries, about 30 had population control programs, another 30 had information and social welfare programs, and about 50 had no population limitation programs at all.[11] This UN conference ended with no explicit consensus among the participants that there was a world population problem at all. The delegates at the conference did pass a resolution stating that all families have the right to plan their families and that it is the responsibility of governments to make sure all families have the ability to do so.

The ability to control the number and timing of children that a couple has is called family planning. Family planning services provide health care and information on contraceptives. It has been estimated that family planning services are available to about one-third of all couples in developing nations and that one-quarter of all couples uses these services.[12] A world survey on contraceptive practices in the early 1980s indicated that about 50 percent of the women of developing countries wanted no more children.[13] Requests by developing nations for foreign aid to help them control their population growth now, for the first time, exceed the international assistance available for this activity. About 2 percent of the foreign aid budgets of Western European countries, the USA, Canada, and Japan went for population assistance in the early 1980s. In the mid-1980s the US government and private American foundations provided about 40 percent of all foreign aid for population control activities. In real dollars (controlling for inflation), US aid actually decreased during the 1970s.[14]

Mexico is a country which has had rather dramatic success with its family planning program. The government began this program only in 1973, when it had one of the highest birth rates in the world. In that year the annual population growth rate was estimated to be 3.5 percent, while in 1982 it was estimated to be down to 2.5 percent. Besides making contraceptives readily available, the government has mounted a large propaganda campaign using television soap operas, billboards, posters on buses and in subway stations, and spot announcements on radio and television. This campaign has been directed mainly at the urban areas, but in the early 1980s efforts were being made to direct a popular soap opera, which has a strong family planning message, to the countryside where 40 percent of the population still lives.[15] Emigration of young men to the USA who are searching for work, and improvements in the status of women, have also been credited with the dramatic drop in birth rates. Even with this reduction in population growth, however, Mexico's population is expected to double in 40 years.[16]

A few countries have adopted more forceful measures than family planning to try to reduce their population growth. Japan drastically reduced its population growth by legalizing abortion after World War II. India, which had had disappointing results with its voluntary family planning programs, enacted more forceful measures in the mid-1970s, such as the compulsory sterilization of some government workers with more than two children. Several Indian states passed laws requiring sterilization and/or imprisonment for those couples who bore more than two or three children. A male vasectomy program was also vigorously pursued, with transistor radios and money being given as an incentive to those agreeing to have the sterilization operation. Public resentment against these policies mounted and helped lead to the defeat of Prime Minister Indira Gandhi's government in 1977. The Indian government has now returned to voluntary measures to try to limit the growth of its population, which is now increasing by over 1 million a month.

China, which has about one-quarter of the world's population but only about 7 percent of its arable land, has launched a vigorous program to limit its population growth and has drastically reduced its birth rate. For many years the communist government, under the leadership of Mao Zedong, encouraged the growth of the population since Mao believed that in numbers there is strength. The policy was eventually reversed, and the present government hopes to limit the population to 1.2 billion by the year 2000. (A 1982 national census revealed that there were about 1 billion people in the country.) A wide assortment of measures are being used to limit the growth. Contraceptives are widely promoted, sterilization is encouraged, and abortion is readily available. The government, through extensive publicity efforts, is promoting the one-child family as the ideal. Late marriages are strongly encouraged, and couples who have only one child receive better jobs and housing, whereas couples with more than two children are taxed more and receive reduced pay. Sociologist Ronald Freedman describes why the Chinese efforts have been successful:

> the massive Chinese national birth-planning program . . . has been organized through the network of political and social organization which mobilizes the masses of the population in primary groups at their places of work and residence . . . That system is used to promote priority objectives – such as birth planning – by persistent and repetitive messages, discussions, and both peer and authority pressure, which is so awesome in its extent that it is hard for us to comprehend.[17]

Promoting Growth

While most countries now seem to realize the need to limit population growth, a few countries favor increasing their populations. Romania is an example of such a country. The birth rate in Romania fell sharply after World War II to such a point that within a few years the population of the country would actually have started declining. In the mid-1960s the government decided to try to reverse this trend by prohibiting abortions, which was one of the main techniques couples used in the postwar period to limit the size of their families. The birth rate immediately shot up, but within a few years it was nearly back to its previous low as couples found other means to limit their families.

The Soviet Union is concerned about its low birth rate and gives various rewards to couples having large families. Medals have been given to women who have many children and appeals have been made to citizens' patriotism. The government has not yet taken the action Romania took; abortions are still available through the public health services and remain the birth control measure most often used by Soviet women to limit their families. The Soviet government is now especially concerned with the imbalances in the birth rates within the country: the low birth rates of the Russian and other European nationalities in the western part of the country, and the high birth rates of various Asian peoples in the eastern part of the country. The Russians are the dominant political force in the country at present. The new demographic situation could produce a very delicate political problem for the government in the future if the people in the eastern republics demand a larger voice in running the government.

The military governments that ruled in Argentina and Brazil in the 1960s and 1970s favored an expansion of their populations. Both countries have large areas which are still sparsely populated, and both are rivals for the role of being the dominant power in Latin America. A few Brazilian military officers even advocated encouraging population growth so that Brazil could pass the USA in size and become the dominant nation in the Western Hemisphere. It is doubtful that more people could ever put Brazil in this position unless the economy makes great advances. A major region of the country with relatively dense population already – the northeast – is one of the poorest areas in the world, and vast tracts of Brazilian land, such as in the Amazon River basin, cannot support large populations.

Other countries, such as Mongolia and those in Africa south of the Sahara, have advocated larger populations both for strategic reasons and because of the belief that a large population is necessary for economic development. Even the US government, which generally recognizes the need for a check on population growth, has some policies which promote large families, such as income tax laws which allow deductions for children and which tax married people at lower rates than single people. Many developed nations have contradictory policies, some encouraging population growth and some discouraging. Some developing nations also have such contradictions, although the greater agreement now in these countries for the need to limit growth often causes these contradictions to be exposed and eliminated.

A generalization that can be made about governmental policies which are aimed at influencing population growth is that, aside from drastic measures, governmental policies have not been very successful in either promoting or limiting birth rates if these policies are out of line with what the population desires. One can also generalize that around the world matters pertaining to reproduction are still considered to be basically the subject for private decisions and not yet matters for public policy to control.

THE FUTURE

The Stabilization of the World's Population

The United Nations predicts that the world's population could stabilize between 8 and 14 billion, depending on the success of efforts to control population growth. The most likely total, according to the UN, is 10.2 billion which will be reached around the year 2100. The UN bases its prediction on the assumption that the world's population growth rates will continue the decline which started in the late 1960s.[18]

The US Bureau of the Census predicts that zero population growth will be reached in the USA around the year 2050, when the population will reach a high of 310 million (in 1985 it was estimated to be 240 million) and then start to decline.[19]

The Carrying Capacity of the Earth

Will the earth be able to support a population of 10 billion, or will catastrophe strike before that figure is reached? Understanding the concept of "carrying capacity" helps one to consider possible answers to that question. Carrying capacity is the maximum number of individuals of a certain species that can be supported by a particular environment. There are four basic relationships that can exist between a growing population and the carrying capacity of the environment in which it exists. A simplified depiction of these is given in figure 5.

In panel A you have a continuously growing carrying capacity and population. This situation is not considered to be relevant to the earth's human beings since several of the resources essential to our survival are finite. Because of this, the carrying capacity of the earth cannot continue indefinitely to grow, although – mainly because of advances in agriculture – it has grown much beyond that foreseen by Robert Malthus, who wrote of the dangers of overpopulation in the late 1700s. Essential resources for humans would include air, energy, food, space, non-renewable resources, heat, and water. Although the potential for increasing the supply of some of these, such as food, still exists, others are limited and

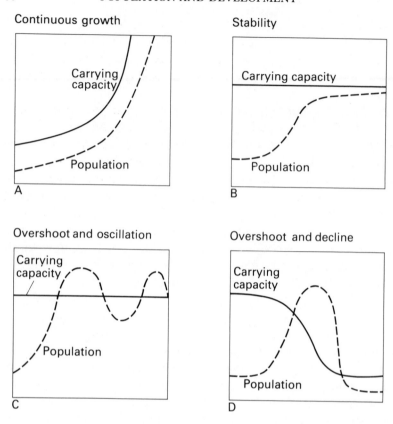

Figure 5 A growing population and carrying capacity

beyond human capacity to expand – now or in the foreseeable future. A basic ecological law is that the size of a population is limited by that resource needed for survival which is in shortest supply. The scarcity of only one of the essential resources for humans would be enough to put a limit on its population growth.

In panel B of figure 5 you have a stable situation since the population has stabilized somewhat below the carrying capacity. Examples of this would appear to be the English sparrow, starling, pheasant, and common city pigeon in the USA. After they were introduced into North America by European settlers they expanded rapidly, often at the expense of native species of birds, but now they have achieved, or are achieving, stable populations.[20] Panel C portrays a situation where the population has overshot the carrying capacity of the environment and then oscillates above and below it. An example of this situation may be that of the lemmings in Alaska. It was observed over a 20-year period that the population of this rodent oscillated sharply along with the availability and health of plants in the arctic tundra. (Some researchers believe that this oscillation may be caused by internal genetic factors within the lemmings rather than by their exceeding the environment's carrying capacity.[21] In panel D we see a situation in which the overshooting of the carrying capacity leads to a precipitous decline in the population, or even to its extinction, and also to a decline in the carrying capacity. Such a situation has occurred with deer on the north rim of the Grand Canyon[22] and with goats in the Middle East. In both of these cases, the number of animals increased to a point where they destroyed the vegetation they fed upon.

It is hoped that the human species with its unique mental powers will follow the situation portrayed in panel B, but there are many indications that the species has not yet recognized its danger and is not yet making effective efforts to prevent either situation C – which would mean the death of millions – or situation D, which could lead to the decline of the human race. There are places in the world, such as sub-Sahara Africa and the Himalaya mountain area, where population expansion has already passed the carrying capacity of the land and the land itself is now being destroyed; fertile land is turning into desert in the African case and land is being destroyed by man-made erosion and floods in the Himalayan case. There are many other examples of the reduction of the carrying capacity of the earth which is taking place at unprecedented rates today around the world – such as over-grazing, over-fishing, over-planting, over-cutting of forests, and the over-production of waste which leads to pollution. (Some of this reduction of carrying capacity is being caused by population pressures and some by economic forces, e.g., the desire to increase profits.) This deterioration has led many ecologists to believe that, unless there is a rapid and dramatic change in many governmental policies, the human species may indeed be headed for the situations depicted in either the oscillation or decline panels above.

Optimum Size of the Earth's Population

What is the optimum size of the earth's population? That question, like others we have asked in this chapter, is not an easy one to answer, but it is worth asking. Paul Ehrlich, the author of *The Population Bomb*, defines the optimum size of the earth's population as that "below which well-being per person is increased by further growth and above which well-being per person is decreased by further growth." What does "well-being" mean? Ehrlich explains what he believes it means:

> The physical necessities – food, water, clothing, shelter, a healthful environment – are indispensable ingredients of well-being. A population too large and too poor to be supplied adequately with them has exceeded the optimum, regardless of whatever other aspects of well-being might, in theory, be enhanced by further growth. Similarly, a population so large that it can be supplied with physical necessities only by the rapid consumption of nonrenewable resources or by activities that irreversibly degrade the environment has also exceeded the optimum, for it is reducing Earth's carrying capacity for future generations.[23]

Ehrlich believes that, given the present patterns of human behavior – behavior which includes the grossly unequal distribution of essential commodities such as food and the misuse of the environment – and the present level of technology, we have already passed the optimum size of population for this planet. Interestingly, a group of scientists in China have come to a similar conclusion regarding their own country. They have concluded that the most suitable population for China in 100 years would be about 650–700 million, about a third below the current population. This reduction could be achieved only if the one-child family is maintained for the next 75 years.[24]

Population-related Problems in our Future

Throughout this book we are going to be looking at many current problems which overpopulation causes or of which it is one of the causes. Here I will mention just a few of the most important ones. Hunger is an obvious problem in which overpopulation plays a key role, and the number of hungry people is undoubtedly increasing. The news media are used to dramatizing this problem only when there are many children with bloated bellies to be photographed, but much more common than the starving child today, and probably in the future, will be the child or adult who is permanently debilitated or who dies because of malnutrition-related diseases. Pollution and the depletion of nonrenewable resources will increase as the world's population grows. Migration of people to lands which do not want them will probably increase in the future and this would cause international tension. The Environmental Fund estimated that in 1980 about 30 percent of the population growth in the USA was coming from illegal immigration, many of whom are Mexicans looking for work.[25] Another possible example of what we might expect to see in the future is the massacre of several thousand unwanted immigrants in Assam, India, which occurred in 1983. Wars have taken place in the past in which overpopulation played an important role and they will probably occur in the future. In the 1960s a border war broke out between El Salvador and Honduras over unwanted Salvadorians in Honduras.

A final problem might be the decline of our civilization because of population pressure. Recent research into the mysterious collapse of the Mayan civilization in Central America suggests that an exponentially growing population may have put pressures on the environment which led to the collapse.[26]

CONCLUSIONS

How should I end this chapter? As I look over the statements by a number of population experts, they seem to share the conclusion that the earth faces an awesome problem with its current population growth of 1 million people every four to five days. This is a problem that is second only to the threat of nuclear war for having the potential for causing untold human misery. But many of these experts also emphasize that human thinking and governmental policies are starting to change and that some impressive reductions in birth rates are taking place in a few countries. Rather than trying to be optimistic or pessimistic at the end, I would like to be realistic. Lester Brown, I believe, states the realism of our situation as well as any:

> Some dimensions of the population problem are economic, some are social, some are ecological, and some are political, but nearly all have one thing in common: they can be expected to get much worse before they get better.[27]

NOTES

1 Council on Environmental Quality and the Department of State, *The Global 2000 Report to the President: Entering the Twenty-first Century*, vol. 1 (Washington, DC: US Government Printing Office, 1980), p.12.
2 *The New York Times*, national edn (October 17, 1985), p. 3.
3 Lester R. Brown, *The Twenty-ninth Day* (New York: W. W. Norton, 1978), p. 73.
4 Paul R. Ehrlich, Anne H. Ehrlich, and John P. Holdren, *Ecoscience: Population, Resources, Environment* (San Francisco: W. H. Freeman, 1977), p. 777.
5 Cited in Ehrlich et al., *Ecoscience*, pp. 777–8.
6 Brown, *Twenty-ninth Day*, p. 77.
7 National Research Council, *Population Growth and Economic Development: Policy Questions* (Washington, DC: National Academy Press, 1986), p. 90.
8 *The New York Times*, late city edn (November 17, 1980), p. A20.
9 *The New York Times*, late city edn (March 9, 1981), p. A21.
10 Brown, *Twenty-ninth Day*, p. 275.
11 *The New York Times*, late city edn (August 18, 1974), p. 2.
12 Council on Environmental Quality and the Department of State, *Global Future: Time to Act* (Washington, DC: US Government Printing Office, 1981), p. 4.
13 Population Action Council, *Popline*, 4 (August 1982), p. 1.
14 Thomas W. Merrick, "World Population in Transition," *Population Bulletin*, 41 (April 1986), p. 34.
15 *The New York Times*, late city edn (January 5, 1982), p. A2.
16 Population Reference Bureau, *1982 World Population Data Sheet*, (Washington, DC: Population Reference Bureau, 1982). Forty years to double the population is longer than one would expect, given

Mexico's present birth rate. This projection is based on reasonable assumptions regarding future birth and death rates.

17 Ronald Freedman, "Theories of Fertility Decline: A Reappraisal," in Philip M. Hauser (ed.), *World Population and Development* (Syracuse, NY: Syracuse University Press, 1979), p. 75.

18 Merrick, "World Population in Transition," pp. 14, 48.

19 *The New York Times*, late city edn (November 9, 1982), p. A19.

20 Burton S. Guttman and John W. Hopkins III, *Understanding Biology* (New York: Harcourt Brace Jovanovich, 1983), p. 745.

21 Amos Turk, et al., *Environmental Science*, 2nd edn (Philadelphia: W. B. Saunders, 1978), pp. 74–6.

22 Edward J. Kormondy, *Concepts of Ecology*, 2nd edn (Englewood Cliffs, NJ: Prentice-Hall, 1976), pp. 111–12.

23 Ehrlich et al., *Ecoscience*, p. 716.

24 *The New York Times*, late city edn (March 15, 1982), p. A6.

25 Environmental Fund, *The Other Side*, no. 22 (Spring 1981), p. 1.

26 E. S. Deevey et al., "Mayan Urbanism: Impact on a Tropical Karst Environment," *Science*, 206 (October 19, 1979), pp. 298–306, and *The New York Times*, late city edn (October 23, 1979), p. C1.

27 Brown, *Twenty-ninth Day*, p. 77.

3

Food and Development

The human brain, so frail, so perishable, so full of
inexhaustible dreams and hungers, burns by the power
of the leaf.
Loren Eiseley (1907–1977), *The Unexpected Universe*

A civilization can be judged by its success in reducing suffering.
This can also be used to judge development. Is it reducing the
misery which exists in the world? Throughout human history,
hunger has caused untold suffering. Because food is a basic
necessity, when it is absent or scarce humans need to spend most of
their efforts trying to obtain it; if they are not successful in finding
adequate food, they suffer and, of course, can eventually die. In the
USA, where dieting is a major concern, there is a tendency to
ignore the problem of hunger. It is so far removed from the daily
experience of most of us that we tend to forget it is a problem for
many in the world. In this chapter we will look at this problem and
also at one closer to home: how our own development affects the
food we eat.

FOOD PRODUCTION

How much food exists in the world at present? Is there enough for
everyone? The answer, which may surprise you, is that, yes, there
is enough. There is enough grain grown in the world today to
provide every man, woman, and child with 3,000 calories a day,
which is only a little less than that consumed by the average person
in the industrialized countries and well above the minimum
requirement for humans.[1] Between the mid-1960s and the mid-

1980s, the production of wheat and feed grains in the world doubled as improved seeds, machinery, fertilizers, and pesticides were used to increase production and new land was cultivated. This impressive performance was counterbalanced, however, by the rapid growth of population which was also taking place in the world at this time. But food production increased rapidly enough in the 1960s and 1970s so that, even with the high rates of population growth in many Third World countries, output of food in the world increased slightly faster than population growth.[2] It was only in Africa that there was a decline in the per capita food output in these two decades (more than 10 percent), because of poor performance in agriculture and very rapid population growth.[3]

HOW MANY ARE HUNGRY?

Unprecedented amounts of food in the world and improving per capita figures do not mean, unfortunately, that everyone is getting enough food. No one knows for sure how widespread hunger is today.[4] Estimates vary from about 450 million hungry to about 1 billion.[5] Actual starvation is rarer today than it has been in the past. Famines still occur because of sudden political upheavals, such as in Cambodia in 1979 and 1980, or partly because of natural disasters, such as droughts in the Sahel region of Africa in the early 1970s and in sub-Sahara Africa in the mid-1980s; however, because of improved communications and transportation, international aid usually mitigates the disaster. A much larger number of people die today because of malnutrition, a malnutrition which weakens them and makes them susceptible to many diseases.

Who are the hungry and where do they live? The answer to the first part of the question is that, according to World Bank estimates, 80 percent are women and children. Malnutrition is common among the poor in many developing countries, and most of these people live in small villages. Because the men are needed to acquire food for the family, they are fed the best. One private American organization working to alleviate world hunger has estimated that about 40 percent of the hungry are landless tenant farmers and agricultural workers, another 40 percent are subsistence farmers, and the final 20 percent live in urban slums.[6] Here is how some of the poor eat in Calcutta, as described by an American journalist who happened to share a meal with them:

> Ahmed . . . invited me for tea at the kiosk, where he shined shoes. A monsoon storm broke, and about a dozen of us ended up spending an hour or two talking together. All of them were either shoeshine men, beggars, or pickpockets. Chowringhee Road was their universe. A meal was served in a big tiffin (luncheon) can. It was rice and curry mixed together – leftovers scraped off the plates at a nearby government canteen by some enterprising Bengali. One portion cost about five cents. It was dumped in a big pile on a newspaper and everyone squatted around in a circle, avidly eating with his fingers.[7]

About one-half of what the World Bank has called the "absolute poor" (those with so little money, goods, and hope to put them in a special class) live in India, Bangladesh, and Pakistan. A large number of them live in Indonesia and in sub-Sahara Africa. The rest are scattered throughout the Middle East, Latin America, and the Caribbean.[8]

There are indications that the number of hunger-related deaths in the world has decreased during the past 30 years in spite of the world's growing population. It is now estimated that about 15 million people die each year from hunger-related causes.[9]

CAUSES OF WORLD HUNGER

If there is more than enough food being grown at present for the world's population but up to a quarter of the earth's people are malnourished, what is causing hunger in the world? Food authorities generally agree that poverty is the main cause of world hunger. Millions of people do not have enough money to buy as much food as they need, or better kinds of food. This is the reason one food expert has written that "Malnutrition and starvation continue more or less unchanged through periods of world food glut and food shortage."[10] The world's poorest cannot afford to purchase the food they need, whatever its price. Other low-income people in the Third World suffer during food shortages when the price of food increases dramatically, as it did during the early

1970s, when world prices of rice, wheat, and corn doubled in just two years. The poor traditionally spend 60–80 percent of their income on food. If world demand is high for certain foods, such as beef for the US fast-food market, then the large landowners in Third World countries grow food or raise cattle for export rather than for domestic consumption. This tends to cause domestic food prices to increase since the supply of local foods is reduced. Much land was being used to grow export crops such as cotton and peanuts in the Sahel, a huge area in Africa just south of the Sahara desert, when a famine hit that area in the early 1970s. Six years of drought, rapid population growth, and misuse of the land led to widespread crop failures and livestock deaths. It is estimated that between 200,000 and 300,000 people starved to death before international aid reached them.[11]

Famine also hit Cambodia in the 1970s. Years of international and civil war, coupled with the genocidal policies of the communist government under the leadership of Pol Pot, led to an estimated 10,000–15,000 people dying per day during the worst of the famine in 1979. A highly successful international aid effort, first organized by private organizations and then joined by governmental agencies, saved the Cambodian people from being destroyed.

Famine hit again in Africa in the mid-1980s. Television pictures of starving people in Ethiopia led to a large international effort by private organizations and by governments to provide food aid. The famine in Ethiopia and in other sub-Saharan African countries was not caused only by the return of a serious drought to the region. Many of the causes of this famine were the same as those which brought on the famine in Africa in the early 1970s. In addition to the reasons stated above, the extensive poverty in the region, a world-wide recession which seriously hurt the export-oriented economies of the African countries, political instability, and governmental development policies that placed a low priority on agriculture have been identified as likely causes.[12]

It is easier to pinpoint the reasons for the famines than for the global malnutrition which exists. Let's look at Bangladesh, which has been called an "international basket case" by some commentators. Its situation is indeed desperate. In a country about the size of the state of Wisconsin (which has a population of 5 million) live about 90 million people. It is one of the most densely populated countries on earth, has one of the highest birth rates, and is one of the poorest. Nutritionists state that the average consumption of food is barely above the starvation level.[13] Yet its land is green and lush and Bangladesh has some of the most fertile soil on the planet. It has plenty of water, and, aside from frequent devastating storms, has a climate which can support three harvests a year. According to some studies, there is probably enough food grown there now to feed the present population adequately, and enough could be grown even to provide for the large increase in population which will take place there in the next 20 years. So what is causing the hunger in Bangladesh? According to the above studies, the feudal economic and social systems are mainly to blame. There is a very unequal distribution of land, with the wealthiest 17 percent of the rural population owning two-thirds of the land. Nearly 60 percent of the rural population owns less than one acre of land, and, with the rapid population growth, the number who own no land at all is growing. The average rural wage is about 50 cents a day. Absentee landlordism is common, and since landlords have major influence in the government, it is unlikely that serious land reform measures will be passed.[14]

According to a study of world hunger which went to the US President in 1980, the developing and developed nations must share the blame for allowing world hunger to exist. Here is what the report of the Presidential Commission said about the responsibility of the developing nations:

In the developing countries, domestic political problems, national security questions, and industrial development generally have attracted more attention and resources than alleviating poverty or investing in agriculture. In fact, few nations have even made these latter concerns top developmental priorities. The development of remote, backward rural areas has had little political or psychological appeal to civilian or military rulers bent on maintaining their control and modernizing their societies along sophisticated technological and industrial lines. Adopting the priorities of the industrialized world, many Third World leaders have modernized their armies and parts of their cities at the expense of their agriculture, health care, and education.

The Commission stated that the USA and other developed nations must share the responsibility for world hunger because their foreign aid policies have been focused in other directions.

> The United States and other developed nations, too, have placed a low priority on alleviating world hunger. Since World War II, the industrialized countries have been preoccupied with East–West tensions and sustaining domestic economic growth. These primary concerns have largely determined both the nature and extent of the West's involvement with the developing world. With national security and anti-Communism as paramount concerns, more money has always been available for military assistance, arms transfers, and the training of military personnel than for educating teachers, scientists, economists, farmers, and health care specialists . . . The hard reality is that the overwhelming majority of the world's hungry people live in countries which have been of limited significance to world grain markets and to Western geopolitical concerns.[15]

The Commission concluded that "the issue of ending world hunger comes down to a question of political choice . . . The Commission agrees with other studies that, if the appropriate political choices were made, the world can overcome the worst aspects of hunger and malnutrition by the year 2000."[16]

FOOD AFFECTS DEVELOPMENT

The availability of food has a direct effect on a country's development. Possibly the most destructive and long-lasting is the effect that the absence of food – or, more often, of the right kinds of food – has on the children of the less developed nations. As mentioned in chapter 2, the dying of many children in poor nations at birth or in their first few years is one of the causes of high birth rates. The UN estimates that about one-half of the children under five in the typical less developed nation suffer from some form of malnutrition.[17] A deficiency of vitamin A leads to blindness of about 100,000 children a year in developing countries.[18] More common than blindness are the harmful effects malnutrition has on the mental development of the children. Eighty percent of the development of the human brain occurs before birth and during the first two years after birth. Malnutrition of the pregnant mother or of the child after birth can adversely affect the child's brain development and, along with the reduced mental stimulation which is common in poor homes, can lead to a reduced capacity for learning.

Malnutrition also reduces a person's ability to ward off diseases since it reduces the body's natural resistance to infection. Measles and diarrhea, which are generally non-serious illnesses in the developed nations, often lead to the death of children in the developing nations; in fact, diarrhea is the single greatest cause of death of children in the Third World. When a child has been weakened by malnutrition, sickness is likely to come more frequently and to be more serious than that experienced by the well-nourished child.

Some Americans, when they first visit the Third World, come away with a feeling that the people are lazy since they are likely to see a number of people sitting around, not doing much of anything. Aside from the absence of jobs or of land they can farm, malnutrition also may be playing a role here because, as one study has stated, "Chronically undernourished people, who commonly also suffer from parasitism and disease, are typically apathetic, listless, and unproductive."[19]

The presence of unhealthy and unproductive people in rural areas probably means that not as much food is being grown as is possible, and the presence of unhealthy and unproductive people in urban areas probably means that not as many manufactured goods and services are being produced. A nation that must spend scarce foreign exchange to buy imported food cannot use those funds to support its development plans. And, more importantly, a nation whose main and most important resource – its people – is weakened by malnutrition is unlikely to generate the kind of economic development which actually does lead to an improved life for the majority of its people. James Grant, the head of the United Nations Children's Fund (UNICEF), has described well the interrelatedness of all key elements of development:

A cat's cradle of . . . synergisms links almost every aspect of development: female literacy catalyzes family planning programmes; less frequent pregnancies improves maternal and child health; improved health makes the most of pre-school or primary education; education can increase incomes and agricultural productivity; better incomes or better food reduces infant mortality; fewer child deaths tend to lead to fewer births; smaller families improve maternal health; healthy mothers have healthier babies; healthier babies demand more attention; stimulation helps mental growth; more alert children do better at school . . . and so it continues in an endless pattern of either mutually reinforcing or mutually retarding relations which can minimize or multiply the benefits of any given input.[20]

DEVELOPMENT AFFECTS FOOD

The development that took place in Europe and the USA as they industrialized led to an increase in the average family's income, and this meant more money to buy food. As we saw in the preceding section, poverty is the main cause of malnutrition. As incomes rose in the West, hunger disappeared as a concern for the average person. Except for some subgroups in Western countries, malnutrition is no longer a common problem.

Development also affects food in other ways. As a nation develops, major changes start to take place in its agriculture. We will look first at how development affects the amount of food that is produced and how it is produced, and then at the way development affects the types of food people eat.

The Production of Food

Western agriculture produces an impressive amount of food. The American supermarket, better than any other institution, illustrates the abundance which modern agriculture can produce. The USA produces so much food that huge amounts of important crops such as corn, wheat, and soybeans are exported. Much of the American abundance has come since the end of World War II. Since 1950, US food production has increased by 50 percent despite a decrease in the land under cultivation.[21] Table 4 shows that, according to an estimate of the US Department of Agriculture, the average American farmer in the early 1980s was producing enough food for 78 people. What is the reason for this increase in production? There are many reasons, of course, but basically, it is because American agriculture has become mechanized and scientific. By using new seeds which can benefit from generous amounts of fertilizer, pesticides, heavy machinery, and irrigation, production has soared. But this accomplishment has had its costs, as we shall see below.

Table 4 Number of people for whom food is produced by each American farm worker

	No. of people
1930	10
1940	11
1950	15
1957	23
1981	78

Source: Data from Wayne Rasmussen and Paul Stone, "Toward a Third Agricultural Revolution," *Food Policy and Farm Programs: Proceedings of the Academy of Political Science*, 34 (1982), p. 183.

Western agriculture basically turns fossil fuel into food. This type of agriculture was developed when oil was inexpensive. Large amounts of energy are needed to build and operate the farm machinery, to build and operate the irrigation systems, to create the pesticides, and to mine and manufacture the fertilizers. Also, huge amounts of energy are needed to process the foods, to transport them to market, to package them, and to display them in retail stores. (Even in this period of greatly increased energy prices, the open freezer in American supermarkets is still common.) It has been estimated that to raise the rest of the world's diet to the American level – especially one featuring its high consumption of beef – would consume nearly all the world's known reserves of oil in 15 years.[22] Figure 6 shows the amount of energy that is needed to produce various foods, and illustrates well the different amounts of

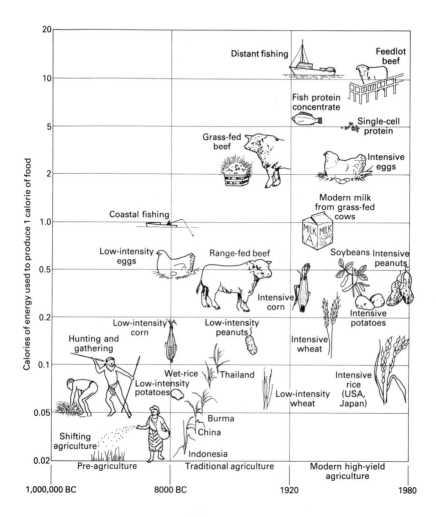

Figure 6 Energy used to produce various foods.

Source: Adapted from *Ecoscience: Population, Resources, Environment* by Paul R. Enrlich et al, p. 349. Copyright © 1970, 1972, 1977 W. H. Freeman and Company. Used by Permission.

energy expended in modern high-yield agriculture in comparison with traditional agriculture and pre-agriculture. The figure shows that important modern foods, such as ocean fish and much of our beef and eggs, actually require an investment of more energy to produce the food than is obtained through the food.

Although modern, mechanized agriculture is generally – but not always – much more productive than the traditional agriculture more commonly found in Third World countries, traditional agriculture is generally far more energy-efficient than Western agriculture. In traditional agriculture the amount of energy used in the form of farm labor and materials is typically small compared with the yield. Returns up to 50 to 1 are possible, although more common are 15 to 1 returns, whereas in modern industrial agriculture more energy is expended than produced.[23] To produce and deliver one can of corn which has 270 calories in it to consumers in the USA, a total of about 2,800 calories of energy must be used. To produce about 4 ounces of beefsteak, which also provides about 270 calories, an astounding 22,000 calories of energy are expended.[24] Anthropologists Peter Farb and George Armelagos give us one perspective we need in order to judge the effects development, as achieved in the West, is having on agriculture:

In short, present-day agriculture is much less efficient than traditional irrigation methods that have been used by Asians, among others, in this century and by Mayans, Mesopotamians, Egyptians, and Chinese in antiquity. The primary advantage of a mechanized agriculture is that it requires the participation of fewer farmers, but for that the price paid in machines, fossil fuels, and other expenditures of energy is enormous.[25]

As the late Barbara Ward, a respected British author of many books on development, noted, "the high-energy [American] food system is one reason why the United States, for 5 percent of the world's people, is now consuming nearly 40 percent of its nonrenewable resources."[26] That statement, more than any other, presents the main argument of those who maintain that there is no way the rest of the world can adopt the agricultural methods followed by the USA at present.

Another feature of American agriculture is an increase in the size

Table 5 Number and size of American farms

	No. of farms	Av. size of farms (acres)
1940	6,000,000	167
1950	5,400,000	213
1981	2,400,000	430

Source: Data from Wayne Rasmussen and Paul Stone, "Toward a Third Agricultural Revolution," *Food Policy and Farm Programs: Proceedings of the Academy of Political Science*, 34 (1982), p. 182.

of farms and a reduction in their number. Table 5 shows how farm size and numbers have changed from 1940 to 1981.

Increased demand for farm products, along with government price supports, enabled farmers to replace old sources of power (horses and mules) with new sources (first the steam engine and then the gasoline engine) and to begin using more machinery, improved seeds, fertilizers, and chemicals to control pests. Dramatic increases in farm productivity resulted, so that by 1981 only about 3 percent of Americans were farmers, down from about 30 percent in 1920.[27] With the increasing financial investment necessary to support the new type of agriculture, and the competition the large farms provide, there has been a noticeable decline in the small, family-owned farm in America.

The growth of what has become known as "agribusiness" – farms run like a big business – has meant an increased concentration of control over the production of food in the USA although there is still sufficient competition in agriculture so that food in the USA remains relatively inexpensive. The large industrial farms can produce harvests of 100 million tomatoes, but sometimes with less efficiency than small operators can obtain. When committees make decisions instead of the farmer growing the crop, when there is inattention to detail, and when there is a lack of dedication – dedication which usually comes only when someone has a personal stake in the farm – one often finds waste and mismanagement. This has happened on large state-owned farms in the Soviet Union, and it is happening on large industrial farms in the USA. When the author of a book on three different types of farms in America saw an entire crop of carrots being plowed under instead of being harvested on a corporation-owned farm in California, he was given the following explanation by a farm supervisor:

> There are enough carrots on [sic] the world right now without these . . . Price isn't so hot, and the warehouses were full when these got to the right size. We were held off harvesting. Someone let time go by and suddenly they were too big. More than eighty acres of them, which comes to sixty million carrots or so. They couldn't fit into those plastic carrot sacks they sell carrots in unless they were cut, and that would have cost the processor a bundle. They offered us a hundred and twenty-five dollars an acre for the carrots – and it would have run us two hundred dollars just to have them contract-harvested. So this is the cheapest alternative . . .[28]

An abundance of food in developed nations seems to lead to increased waste. It has been estimated by a congressional report that, yearly, the USA throws away enough food to feed about 50 million people.[29]

Besides the waste of food, there is another waste occurring in the USA which could affect profoundly its ability to produce food in the future: this deals with the loss of farmland.

About 3 million acres of farmland in the USA is being lost annually because of development; it's being covered over by houses, roads, shopping centers, factories, and by general urban sprawl. While the amount lost is small compared with the amount of actual and potential cropland in the USA (about 0.5 percent), the land lost is often prime farmland, and it can be replaced only by marginal land, which is not as fertile, is more open to erosion, and is more costly to use.[30] Other land is being lost in the USA because of overplanting and erosion. The planting, year after year, of certain export crops drains the soil of valuable nutrients. Also, farmers in the West are starting to plow up fragile prairie and other grasslands to grow wheat for export. Windbreaks of trees which were planted during the Dust Bowl years of the 1930s are being cut down to provide more land for wheat. The USA has already lost about one-third of the topsoil of its productive farmland.[31] But a study published by the National Academy of Sciences in the mid-1980s concluded that soil erosion in the USA was unlikely to harm crop productivity in the twenty-first century. The study found that about 75 percent of the nation's cropland was eroding at low enough rates so that the lands could remain productive indefinitely.[32] A law passed by the US Congress in 1985 could continue to improve the situation, as it aims to take about 45 million acres of the most highly erodible land out of production by paying farmers to grow erosion-resistant grass and trees on the land.

The Type of Food

As a nation develops, its diet changes. The wealthier a nation becomes, the more calories and protein its citizens consume. The average citizen of a Western industrialized nation consumes many more calories and much more protein than he or she needs for good health. Much of the excess of protein comes from a large increase in meat consumption. Often the consuming of meat instead of grains in order to get protein, which is needed for human growth and development, is a very inefficient use of food.[33] As figure 7 shows, for every 16 pounds of grain and soybeans fed to beef cattle in the USA about 1 pound of meat for human consumption is obtained. About three-quarters of the food energy in an Asian's diet comes directly from grain (about 300–400 lb a year) whereas an American consumes nearly one ton of grain per year, but 80 percent of it is first fed to animals.[34] The USA consumes the highest amount of meat per person in the world, although many other Western developed nations also have high meat consumption. It is generally agreed by experts on nutrition that excessive calories and excessive meat consumption can lead to serious health problems. Barbara Ward describes the harmful features of such a diet:

The car and the television set and the growing volume of office work may well have produced the most literally sedentary population human society has ever known. But at the same time, diets stuffed with the proteins and calories needed for a lumberman or a professional boxer have become prevalent. Everywhere, high meat consumption demands grain-fed

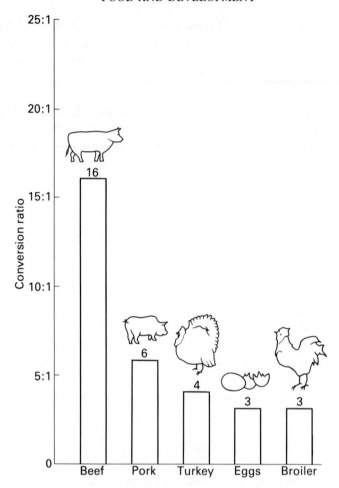

Figure 7 Pounds of grain and soybeans fed to get one pound of meat, poultry, or eggs in the USA.

Source: Frances Lappé, *Diet for a Small Planet* (New York: Ballantine Books, 1982), p. 70. Reprinted by permission of Frances Moore Lappé and her agents, Raines & Raines. Copyright © 1971, 1975, 1982 by Frances Moore Lappé.

animals. Meanwhile, what little grain we do eat through bread usually has little nutritional value and roughage, since these are removed when the flour is refined. Thus, the human bowel is deprived of the fiber it requires to function easily. The eating of fresh vegetables – which also give necessary fiber –

has fallen off by between a third and a half in the last half century. Processed, defibered products have taken their place. The results are literally apparent. In all developed nations, obesity and diet-related illnesses are now a major medical problem . . . Many medical experts are now agreed that, with fat, sugar, cholestrol, refined grains, food additives, and the general absence of roughage, modern citizens are literally – via heart attacks and cancer – eating and drinking themselves into the grave.[35]

I'd like to end this section with a short explanation of how development has affected the first food humans receive after birth. If you were born before 1940, the chances are good that the first food you had was human milk from your mother's breast, whereas if you were born after 1955,[36] your first food was probably a man-made formula from a bottle (using cow's milk as the basic ingredient). A rapid decline in breast-feeding is now taking place in the Third World, in part because of urbanization and the promotional efforts of formula-making companies (more of a factor in the past than at present), and in part because of a desire to imitate the USA, to be "modern." As the poor in the Third World see it, if the rich are bottle-feeding their babies, it must be better.

But is it? No, it's not. Nutritionists agree that human milk is the best food for babies. Breast-feeding is also the safest, cheapest, and easiest way to feed babies. Breast-feeding probably improves bonding – a special feeling of closeness – between the mother and the baby, and, as we saw in chapter 2, it can act as a natural birth control. Breast-feeding gives the baby antibodies which enable it to fight off infection; this is especially important since its own immune system is not fully developed during the first year. A 1980 study in Brazil of children of poor parents showed that bottle-fed babies were three to four times more likely to be malnourished than those who were breast-fed. Studies have also shown that in India bottle-fed babies have diarrhea three times more often than breast-fed babies, and in Egypt infant deaths are five times higher among bottle-fed babies than among breast-fed ones.[37] Many of the harmful effects of bottle-feeding in the Third World occur because of a lack of refrigeration, and of knowledge about the importance of sterilization. Also, the bottled mixture is expensive so poor mothers n dilute it with water, which makes the formula too weak.

There is now a movement by some American mothers to return ɔ breast-feeding, but those who breast-feed their children for at least three months are still in the minority. Working mothers find bottle-feeding more convenient, and the American culture still considers breast-feeding a shocking sight. Because American women can no longer turn to their mothers for help or encouragement in breast-feeding (since their mothers didn't do it), a special organization – La Leche League – has been formed by some American women to help others learn about breast-feeding and to aid them with any difficulties they experience. What we find in this case is a modern society turning away from one of the most basic human functions and then having to relearn the advantages of this bodily function and how to practice it.

The general recognition of the harmful effects which were coming with the adoption of bottle-feeding by Third World nations led the World Health Organization in 1981 to adopt, by a vote of 118 to 1 (only the USA voted "no"), a non-binding code restricting the promotion of infant formula.[38]

THE GREEN REVOLUTION

The bringing of high agricultural technology to the Third World has been called the Green Revolution. The Green Revolution has two basic components: the use of new seeds, especially for wheat, rice, and corn, and the use of various "inputs," such as fertilizer, irrigation, and pesticides. The new seeds, which were developed over 20 years of cross-pollinating, are highly responsive to fertilizer. If they receive sufficient fertilizer and water, and if pests are kept under control, the seeds produce high yields. The introduction of this new agricultural technology to the Third World in the mid-1960s brought greatly increased harvests of wheat and impressive increases in rice production in a number of Asian countries. Over a six-year period, India doubled its wheat production and Pakistan did nearly as well. Significant increases of rice production occurred in the Philippines, Sri Lanka, Indonesia, and Malaysia. Mexico's wheat and corn production tripled in only two decades.[39] Not only were the harvests much larger, but multiple harvests – in some places up to three – became possible in a year because of the fast maturing of the plants.

Unfortunately, the Green Revolution has had some significant unanticipated and negative side-effects. One of the worst, which is discussed more fully in the chapter on technology, is that it has tended to benefit the rich and large farmers in the developing countries much more than the small, poor farmers. Fertilizer, pesticides, irrigation systems, and the new seeds all cost money, and it is the larger farmers who have the wealth to purchase these or the access to credit to finance them.

Other negative aspects of the new technology have become apparent. The new highly inbred seeds are often less resistant to diseases than are some of the traditional seeds. Also, the planting of only one variety of a plant – called monoculture – creates an ideal condition for the rapid spreading of disease or for the rapid multiplying of insects that feed on that plant. (The Irish potato blight in the mid-1800s and the American corn blight of 1970 are examples of serious diseases that have attacked monocultures.) The new seeds are also less tolerant of too little or too much water; thus, droughts and floods have a more harmful impact on these plants than on the traditional varieties of the grains.

Certainly, without the increased production which came with the Green Revolution many developing countries would have already lost the battle to have enough food available for their rapidly growing populations. But as the "father" of the Green Revolution, the American Dr Norman Borlaug – who received the Nobel Peace Prize for his work in developing high-yield wheat – has stated, the Green Revolution was not meant to be the final solution for the world's food problem: it was designed to give nations a breathing space of 20 or 30 years during which time they could work to bring their population growth under control. Borlaug is as disappointed, as many others are, that this time has not been used by many nations to take forceful measures to rein in their exploding numbers.[40]

GOVERNMENTAL FOOD POLICIES

The availability of food is such a basic need that no government that I know of adopts a "hands off" policy regarding its production, price, and distribution. As was mentioned above under the section "Causes of World Hunger," many developing nations have given a relatively low priority to agricultural development and to relieving poverty in the rural areas, concentrating on industrial development instead of rural development. Nearly all of the developing nations have scarce public funds, so decisions must be made about where to apply them. It should not be surprising to students of government that public funds usually go to benefit groups with political visibility and power. Political leaders want to stay in power, and it is often the traditional political and economic elites which will influence the leader's length of stay rather than the scattered and weak – both physically and politically – small farmers and rural poor. The urban masses are much more of a threat to the leaders than the small farmers, and urban people demand plentiful and inexpensive food.

The desire to retain power, of course, is not the only reason why rural development has not been given a high priority in many Third World nations. The desire to achieve the high living standards in the West by following the route taken by the USA and other developed nations – both capitalist and communist – with their emphasis on industrialization has been hard to resist; it has seemed like a relatively fast way to reduce poverty. US foreign aid in the 1950s and 1960s certainly encouraged developing nations along this route. We who were in the foreign aid program then recognized that this development strategy was a gamble, that maybe benefits would not trickle down to the poor; but the other alternative of trying to work directly with the millions of rural poor did not seem viable. Barbara Ward shows how dominant this strategy of emphasizing industrialization over rural development became: "So far, on average, only 20 percent of the investment of most developing nations has gone to the 70 to 80 percent of the people who are in the rural areas."[41]

How does one respond to the argument that, given limited public funds, it is impossible to give any significant aid to the millions in the rural areas where most of the hunger exists? The response is that a few Asian countries – namely, Japan, South Korea, and Taiwan – have brought significant prosperity to their rural areas by doing certain things. First, they enacted land reform measures – in Japan's case, under the US occupation force's direction after World

War II – which ended absentee landlordism and exploitative tenancy arrangements. The land was basically turned over to those who farmed it. Second, cooperatives were established to help small farmers with their purchasing of needed inputs and with the marketing of their harvests. The governments also provided information and aid to the farmers through an active agricultural extension service and by supporting agricultural research. Japanese small farmers now have some of the highest yields per acre in the world, and the mechanization they have used on their farms – mainly small machines – has tended to increase rural employment, not decrease it. Double and even triple harvests per year on the same piece of land became possible, and more laborers were required to handle these harvests.

China under Mao Zedong emphasized agriculture instead of industrialization after the disastrous "Great Leap Forward" (a crash program of economic development in the late 1950s). China has achieved impressive increases in its agricultural production, but because of its rapid population growth the increased food has mainly gone to feed the increased number of people. Hunger is certainly less of a problem in China today than it was before the communist takeover, but the costs have been high. Political opponents have been dealt with harshly and significant damage to the environment came from the efforts to increase the amount of agricultural land. Forests were cut down and marginal pasture land was converted to land for crops. Even though the communist government also made efforts to protect the environment, its actions directed toward increasing agricultural production led to an increased strain on the land. Significant increases in erosion and even possible climate changes (decreased rainfall) have been reported.[42]

Another major communist government – the Soviet Union – pursued radically different policies from China. Under Stalin's long rule, the country placed industrialization first and agriculture was used to support that industrialization. Also, the desire to remove political opponents to the communists' rule – the prosperous small farmers known as the "kulaks" – and the desire to substitute state-owned and collective farms for privately owned farms, has led to what is commonly recognized as the destruction of efficient agriculture in that country. The Soviet Union's inability to grow enough food to feed its people has caused it to import large amounts of wheat from the USA and other capitalist countries.

There is space in this chapter to sketch US food policies only briefly. The main point that should be made is that the US government is very active in this area. Up to the 1900s the government's policy was mainly to encourage farm production, but since the 1950s the policy has been directed mainly at coping with an excess of production. The basic policy has been to prop up low farm incomes by using price supports, by purchasing surpluses, and by paying the farmers to grow less food. During the 1950s and 1960s, the US government's policy (and Canada's) of buying up farm surpluses led to huge public reserves. Food from this reserve often went to poor nations under the Public Law 480 program, whereby surplus food was given or sold to developing nations. World food prices were generally stable during this period since, during bad harvest years, food from the public reserve was released. Now it is no longer the policy of either the USA or Canada to encourage large public food reserves, so reserves no longer can act as a cushion during periods of poor harvests. More recently, the US government has encouraged and supported the export of US farm products to other nations. The USA has become the world's leading exporter of food. The government supports this because, as mentioned above, exports help correct the large trade deficits that the country often experiences. This policy, and the strong political power of the American farmer, helps one to understand why the strongly anti-communist US President in the early 1980s – Ronald Reagan – removed the embargo on selling grain to the Soviet Union which his predecessor had ordered after the USSR invaded Afghanistan in 1979.

FUTURE FOOD SUPPLIES

How much food can be grown in the world? How many can be fed? Like most of the other questions raised in this book, there are no simple answers. Also, it is not hard to find experts who give very different answers to these questions. In this final section we will look at six topics which are directly related to these important questions: the effect of climate, the amount of arable land, energy costs, efforts to increase the efficiency of agriculture, new foods and technology, and, finally, expected future food production.

Climate

Experts disagree about whether the earth is going to have a warmer or colder climate in the future, but they are in general agreement that there will probably be more variability in the climate than there has been in the recent past. There is general agreement that the climate over the past several decades in the USA and Canada has been unusually good for agriculture, but that such good climate cannot be taken for granted. In fact, variability is the hallmark of the earth's climate when it is examined over long periods; one sees long-term cycles of hundreds of years and shorter cycles of 15–20 years.[43] Some of these cycles may be related to solar activity. A greater variability of climate (higher and lower extremes of temperature and higher and lower amounts of rainfall) will probably lower agricultural production around the world because of the large amount of marginal land which is now being used for agriculture. On this land, such as parts of the American West, the Canadian west, and the Soviet east, a slight reduction in rainfall or a slightly shorter growing season can spell the difference between a good harvest and little or no harvest.

Arable Land

About one-half of the world's land which could be cultivated, the arable land, is presently being used for agriculture. Large amounts of potential farmland exist in Latin America and Africa; the UN's Food and Agriculture Organization (FAO) estimates that only about 20 percent of the potentially arable land in these two regions is now being cultivated.[44] Yet the US government's *Global 2000 Report* projects that land being used for agriculture will increase by only 4 percent between 1970 and the year 2000.[45] Why this big difference between the potential and the expected? In Africa much of the unused arable land is infested with the tsetse fly, which causes sleeping sickness. Another important reason is that most of the good farmland in the world is already being used. Much of the remaining arable land is far from population centers, and a lot of it is marginal land, which is costly to bring into production and to maintain. Large amounts of energy would be needed to develop it – to build roads to it and to transport its products to market, to irrigate it, and to fertilize it. Because of these problems, plus the social and political obstacles which must be overcome to develop such areas, it is difficult to estimate the potential for increasing the amount of farmland. But many experts agree that only a modest increase will probably be achieved in the near future. These estimates also must take into consideration the large amount of present farmland which is being lost to agriculture through urbanization, through erosion caused by the cutting down of forests and overcropping, through the spreading of desert-like conditions (desertification) because of overgrazing and farming on the edge of deserts, and through the loss of irrigated lands (salinization and waterlogging) because of poor drainage. The *Global 2000 Report* cites the example of Egypt, where,

despite efforts to open new lands to agriculture, the total area of irrigated farmland has remained almost unchanged in the past two decades. As fast as additional areas are irrigated with water from the Aswan Dam, old producing lands on the Nile are converted to urban uses.[46]

Energy Costs

The dramatic increase in energy costs in the 1970s had a profound influence on agriculture, and expected rising energy costs in the future will strongly affect food production and the cost of food. As we have seen, modern, Western agriculture is energy-intensive, and the spreading of that type of agriculture to the Third World via the Green Revolution also entailed a commitment to using large amounts of energy. Probably more than any other single factor, the cost and availability of energy will strongly affect agricultural production in the future. In the past, a doubling of agricultural output has required a ten-fold increase in the amount of energy used.[47] Some people hope for a breakthrough in nuclear fusion research which could lead to vast amounts of electrical energy becoming available; fossil fuels could then be designated for use in agriculture. Others hope that the Third World will somehow develop an agriculture which does not depend on the high use of energy and energy-related inputs which is common in the developed countries. To do this, it would also have to reject the Western diet as an ideal to be strived for.

Increased Efficiency

If the potential for increasing the amount of farmland in the world is not great and the cost of energy can be expected to rise over the long run – as we shall see in chapter 4 – what hope is there for feeding the world's expanding population? Some see a hope in increasing production by improving farming methods on existing farmland. The FAO estimates that vast increases in farm production could be achieved in the Third World through improved farm techniques.[48] Some of this may be achieved by spreading Green Revolution techniques to new land, but the problems of doing this, as we have seen, remain formidable. Another possibility that is being considered is an increase in organic farming. This type of farming, which is now practiced on only about 1 percent of the world's farms, is designed to conserve energy and natural resources. Pesticides are shunned, and natural fertilizers are used to maintain and improve soil fertility. Whether organic farming or some other technique is adopted – such as used on Japanese farms, where relatively small plots of land are intensely worked – an increase in efficiency on Third World farms could increase production.

New Foods and Technology

Genetic engineering in food plants has been called a technology with the potential to transform agriculture, but no one can predict when it will arrive or how it will affect food production. Research is being conducted on breeding a resistance to diseases and insects, to saline soils and herbicides, and to droughts and extreme temperatures. Another area of research is focused on the winged bean. This highly nutritious bean, like other beans, when combined with corn has the protein value of milk. It can grow on sandy or clay soils without fertilizer, and some agriculturists believe it may become "the soybean of the tropics."

A possibility of increasing the protein available to the world could come from the harvesting of the shrimp-like krill in the Antarctic. Krill, which used to be the main food of some species of whales before they were decimated by overfishing, exist in large numbers. It is also believed that aquaculture, or fish farming, might produce significant amounts of protein in the future.

Future Production of Food

The *Global 2000 Report*[49] projects that world food production will stay ahead of population growth up through the year 2000.

During the period 1970–2000, the Report projects a 90 percent increase in food production which works out as a 15 percent per capita increase in food. (This projection is based on an assumption that there will be no deterioration of climate – an assumption, as we have seen, which may not be justified.) There is great variability among regions of the world, however, with the greatest per capita food increases occurring in those countries, such as the developed nations, which already have high per capita consumption. The large, densely populated countries of South Asia (India, Pakistan, etc.) will improve hardly at all, nor will large areas in the Middle East and North Africa. The Report projects a decline by the year 2000 in per capita food consumption for many less developed nations in Africa south of the Sahara desert.[50]

Not too long ago, many people hoped that the world food problem would be solved by harvesting fish from the oceans; but it is now generally recognized that, as one marine biologist has put it, most of the ocean is a biological desert.[51] Nearly all the fish in the world are harvested in coastal waters and in a relatively few places further from land where there is a strong up-welling of water which brings nutrients to the surface. The world fish catch leveled off in the 1970s. The *Global 2000 Report* projects that the catching of fish in the world will increase little, if at all, by the year 2000.[52]

During the coming decades, there will undoubtedly be chronic local food shortages and periods of general food surplus and shortages. It is expected that a number of countries will grow even more dependent than they are now on a limited number of major grain producers, such as the USA. The *Global 2000 Report* expects that the USA will retain its position as the world's largest food exporter through the year 2000.

Even with world per capita food production increasing, it is expected that, if present trends and governmental policies continue, the number of malnourished people in the world will be greater in the year 2000 than it is now. The World Bank has estimated that the number of malnourished people in the Third World could increase from 400–600 million in the mid-1970s to about 1.3 billion in 2000.[53] One of the reasons for this increase, even with improving per capita figures, is that per capita figures are averages and thus mask great differences among people, with many eating more than they need and many less. But this is only part of the reason. Although the cost of petroleum is not increasing as much as was expected in the late 1970s and early 1980s, the long-term prospect for an increase in the cost of petroleum is still good, and this will probably lead to more expensive food. Agriculture researcher John Tarrant explains how increasing prices will affect the world's food problem:

> The *real* problem that remains is the long-term inability of the world to feed its continuously growing population *at a price that this population can afford to pay*. There is a considerable potential to raise food production in the world, but it will be expensive food. Much of the world's population is too poor to purchase food at its current prices. The problem is not so much the technical fix of increasing food production, although this will get progressively more difficult, but the social and economic development in the Third World which will enable the population to purchase food at all.[54]

CONCLUSIONS

One of the most fundamental problems many less developed nations face is how to end hunger in their lands. The rapid growth of their populations and the past neglect of agricultural development have resulted in increased suffering in rural areas. Advances in technology have helped to keep the overall production of food in many poor countries ahead of their increased needs, but widespread poverty in the rural districts as well as some in urban areas has meant that many people can not afford to purchase the food that exists in the market. The growth-with-equity approach, which was presented in chapter 1, would seem to offer some ways to attack the problem. The emphasis the approach places on agricultural development and on increasing employment in both rural and urban areas should provide increased income to larger numbers of the poor. Japan, South Korea, and Taiwan show that, if certain governmental actions are taken and a basically free market exists, poverty can be drastically reduced.

The developed nations face awesome food problems also. Here the problems are quite different from those faced by the developing nations. The rich nations need to learn how to produce healthful food and to retain a prosperous agricultural sector. There are indications that, among some in the USA, a new concern does exist with the types of food people eat. Whether this desire for more healthful foods and the awareness of the connection between food and health will spread from a minority to the majority of the people is not yet clear. It is clear, though, that in economic systems where consumers can freely exercise their preferences, the potential exists for important changes to occur fairly rapidly.

The picture regarding the health of the farm economy in some developed countries does not look bright. In the USA the large debt which many farmers have incurred has cast a dark cloud over farming. The USA has not yet learned how to maintain a sustaining, prosperous agricultural sector. Its productive capabilities are impressive, but, as this chapter has pointed out, its high dependency on uncertain and potentially very costly energy supplies, and its tendency to undermine the land upon which it rests, make its future uncertain.

NOTES

1 Frances Moore Lappé and Joseph Collins, *Food First: Beyond the Myth of Scarcity*, rev. edn (New York: Ballantine Books, 1978), p. 122; and Raymond Hopkins, Robert Paarlberg, and Mitchel Wallerstein, *Food in the Global Arena* (New York: Holt, Rinehart and Wilson, 1982), p. 2.
2 Barbara Insel, "A World Awash in Grain," *Foreign Affairs*, 63 (Spring 1985), p. 893.

3 Erik P. Eckholm, *Down to Earth: Environment and Human Needs* (New York: W. W. Norton, 1982), pp. 21–2.

4 "Hunger" and "undernourishment" refer to the consumption of insufficient calories, whereas "malnutrition" refers to the lack of some necessary nutrients, usually protein. For the sake of simplicity, I am equating hunger with undernourishment and malnutrition.

5 Nevin Scrimshaw and Lance Taylor, "Food," *Scientific American* (September 1980), p. 80.

6 The Hunger Project, *A Shift in the Wind*, no. 12, p. 9.

7 Richard Critchfield, *Villages* (Garden City, NY: Anchor Press/ Doubleday, 1981), pp. 285–6.

8 Eckholm, *Down to Earth*, p. 15.

9 Roy L. Prosterman, *The Decline in Hunger-related Deaths*, The Hunger Project Papers, no. 1 (San Francisco: The Hunger Project, 1984), p. ii.

10 John R. Tarrant, *Food Policies* (New York: John Wiley, 1980), p. 12.

11 *The New York Times*, late city edn (June 7, 1983), p. 1.

12 For a full discussion of the causes of the African famines see Carl K. Eicher, "Facing Up to Africa's Food Crisis," *Foreign Affairs*, 61 (Fall 1982), pp. 151–74; and a series of articles on Africa in the *Bulletin of the Atomic Scientists*, 41 (September 1985), pp. 21–52.

13 Critchfield, *Villages*, p. 71.

14 Lappé and Collins, *Food First*, pp. 17–23; *The New York Times*, late city edn (November 24, 1981), p. 1.

15 Presidential Commission on World Hunger, *Overcoming World Hunger: The Challenge Ahead* (Washington, DC: US Government Printing Office, 1980), p. 43.

16 Ibid., p. 45.

17 Paul R. Ehrlich, Anne H. Ehrlich, and John P. Holdren, *Ecoscience: Population, Resources, Environment* (San Francisco: W. H. Freeman, 1977), p. 313.

18 Presidential Commission on World Hunger, *Overcoming World Hunger*, p. 16.

19 Ehrlich et al., *Ecoscience*, p. 303.

20 As quoted in The Hunger Project, *A Shift in the Wind*, no. 15, p. 4.

21 *Christian Science Monitor* (April 1, 1982), p. 4.

22 Hopkins et al., *Food in the Global Arena*, p. 102.

23 William Ophuls, *Ecology and the Politics of Scarcity* (San Francisco: W. H. Freeman, 1977), pp. 42–3. The energy expended in modern agriculture is mainly nonhuman energy, of course, and most people consider that to be one of modern agriculture's most attractive features.

24 Peter Farb and George Armelagos, *Consuming Passions: The Anthropology of Eating* (Boston: Houghton Mifflin, 1980), p. 69.

25 Ibid., pp. 69–70.

26 Barbara Ward, *Progress for a Small Planet* (New York: W. W. Norton, 1979), p. 92.

27 Ross Talbot, "Food in the American Political Economy," *Food Policy and Farm Programs: Proceedings of the Academy of Political Science*, 34 (1982), pp. 1–2.

28 Mark Kramer, *Three Farms: Making Milk, Meat and Money from the American Soil* (Boston: Little, Brown, 1980), p. 248.

29 Ward, *Progress for a Small Planet*, p. 93.

30 *Christian Science Monitor* (February 3, 1981), p. 3; (April 1, 1982), p. 4.

31 *Christian Science Monitor* (April 1, 1982), p. 4.

32 *The New York Times*, late city edn (May 16, 1986), p. A10.

33 The consumption of meat (and also, milk from cows and goats) *can* make nutritional sense. Cows and sheep, for example, can consume grasses, which people are unable to digest, in places where climate or the condition of the land makes the growing of crops impossible.

34 Ehrlich et al., *Ecoscience*, p. 315.

35 Ward, *Progress for a Small Planet*, pp. 93–4.

36 Bottle-feeding became more common in the USA than breast-feeding sometime between 1940 and 1955. A lack of good data makes it difficult to pin this down any further.

37 *The New York Times*, national edn (December 17, 1982), p. 8.

38 For a discussion of the controversy over the use of infant formula see Stephen Solomon, "The Controversy Over Infant Formula," *New York Times Magazine* (December 6, 1981), p. 100.

39 Lester R. Brown, *The Twenty-Ninth Day* (New York: W. W. Norton, 1978), pp. 146–7; Peter Steinhart, "The Second Green Revolution," *New York Times Magazine* (October 25, 1981), p. 48.

40 Population Action Council, *Popline*, 4 (August 1982), p. 2.

41 Ward, *Progress for a Small Planet*, p. 178.

42 Vaclav Smil, "Ecological Mismanagement in China," *Bulletin of the Atomic Scientists*, 38 (October 1982), pp. 18–23; *The New York Times*, late city edn (April 7, 1980), p. A12.

43 Tarrant, *Food Policies*, pp. 43 and 279.

44 Ibid., pp. 35–6; *The New York Times*, late city edn. (August 17, 1981), p. D10.

45 Council on Environmental Quality and the Department of State, *The Global 2000 Report to the President: Entering the Twenty-First Century*, vol. 1 (New York: Penguin Books, 1982), p. 16.

46 Ibid., pp. 33, 35.
47 Ophuls, *Ecology and the Politics of Scarcity*, p. 54.
48 *The New York Times*, late city edn (August 17, 1981), p. D10.
49 The *Global 2000 Report* is based on a three-year study by US government agencies of what the world will be like in the year 2000 if present policies and trends continue. The Report makes projections, not predictions; those making the projections recognize that policies and trends can change between now and the year 2000. I have relied primarily on the Report when writing this section on the future production of food because its projections are the most comprehensive that have been made up to now.
50 *Global 2000 Report*, pp. 13–17.
51 Ehrlich et al., *Ecoscience*, p. 353.
52 *Global 2000 Report*, p. 21.
53 Ibid., p. 17.
54 Tarrant, *Food Policies*, p. 295.

4

Energy and Development

A human being, a skyscraper, an automobile, and a blade of grass all represent energy that has been transformed from one state to another.

Jeremy Rifkin, *Entropy*

THE ENERGY CRISIS

Are we running out of energy? Of course not. Everything is made out of energy, and, as college students learn when they study the laws of thermodynamics in their introductory physics courses, energy cannot be destroyed. These laws also state that energy cannot be created: all we can do is to transform it from one state to another. And when energy is so transformed, or in other words when it is used for some work, the energy is changed from a more useful to a less useful form. All types of energy eventually end up as low-grade heat. A "law" in the physical sciences means that there are no exceptions to it, and there are none to the laws of thermodynamics.[1]

So if everything is energy and energy cannot be destroyed, why is there an energy crisis? The crisis has come because of the other aspects of these laws, the parts that tell us that energy cannot be created, and that, once used, it is transformed into a less usable form. At present, the industrialized world relies on a very versatile fuel – oil. Oil is being consumed at prodigious rates, its supply is limited, and its price has fluctuated greatly, increasing dramatically from the mid-1970s to the early 1980s and then falling in the mid-1980s. The developed nations are faced with an energy crisis because the era of cheap oil from reliable sources is over. Table 6

Table 6 US Gasoline prices, 1950–80

	Retail price per gallon of regular gas ($)
1950	0.27
1960	0.31
1970	0.36
1980	1.21

Source: *Dollars and Sense* (July–August 1980); presented in Kenneth Dolbeare, *American Public Policy* (New York: McGraw-Hill, 1982), p. 113.

shows this fact as well as any set of figures can, as it focuses on the changes in the price of gasoline in the USA from 1950 to 1980. The table also helps us to understand another important feature of the energy crisis, especially as it has affected the USA. The period of cheap gasoline was a relatively long one, and Americans got used to having inexpensive petroleum products. Unprecedented economic growth and material prosperity took place in the USA during the 1950s and 1960s, and this was made possible, in part, by cheap energy. Individual life-styles and modes of industrial production were based on plentiful, inexpensive energy, and when oil prices skyrocketed in the 1970s, the shock to the American economy, and to the economies of many other countries, was profound.

The first oil shock took place in 1973–4. The 1973 Arab–Israeli war led a number of Arab oil-producing countries to stop shipping oil to the USA and other countries allied with Israel. American motorists lined up at gas stations, vying for limited supplies. The Organization of Petroleum Exporting Countries (OPEC), of which most oil-exporting nations are members, seized the opportunity to raise oil prices significantly: they quadrupled.

The second oil shock came in 1979–80. The event which prompted this shock was the Iranian revolution and the ousting of the Shah as the head of the Iranian government. Iranian oil shipments to the USA stopped, but the real shock came when OPEC doubled its prices. Many Americans had refused to believe there was a real energy crisis after the first oil shock and had returned to their normal high consumption of petroleum products after the Arab embargo was lifted; but the second oil shock convinced most people that there was indeed an energy crisis. While many had blamed either the American oil companies or the US government for creating the first oil crisis, the second shock clearly demonstrated that something had fundamentally changed in the world. What became apparent to many now was that the USA, and most other developed nations, were dependent on one section of the world for a significant part of their energy, and that they could no longer control events in that part of the world.

The Middle East, where much of the oil imported into the USA and Western Europe comes from, is a highly unstable area. It is torn by regional conflicts (the Arabs against Israel, Iran against Iraq, Syria against Iraq, Egypt against Libya); by religious conflicts (Moslem against Jew, Christian against Moslem, Shi'ite Moslem against Sunni Moslem); by social and ideological conflicts (traditionalists against radicals); and by East–West competition (the USA against the Soviet Union). A large amount of the oil which is involved in international trade is carried on ships which must pass through a single strait in the Persian Gulf – the Strait of Hormuz.[2]

The USA is the largest buyer of oil in the world, with much of it coming from a single country, Saudi Arabia. But many Western European countries are even more dependent on imported oil than is the USA, and Japan is the industrialized country most dependent on imported oil, producing virtually no oil itself and having few other domestic sources of energy.[3]

The large increases in the price of oil by OPEC in the 1970s led to a massive transfer of wealth from the developed nations to part of the Third World. In the words of one commentator, "It may represent the quickest massive transfer of wealth among societies since the Spanish Conquistadores seized the Incan gold stores some four centuries ago."[4] Higher oil prices led to low economic growth, higher inflation, big trade deficits, and increased unemployment in the USA and other developed nations. Although developing nations use much less oil than do the developed nations, the cost of their imported oil also went up and caused some of them to acquire huge debts to pay for this necessary resource. Daniel Yergin, one of the co-editors of an important report on energy by the Harvard Business School, assessed the potential consequences of the oil shocks in the following terms:

The unhappy set of economic circumstances set in motion by the oil shocks contains the potential for far-reaching crises. In the industrial nations, high inflation, low growth, and high unemployment can erode the national consensus and undermine the stability and legitimacy of the political system. In the developing world, zero growth leads to misery and upheavals. Protectionism and accumulation of debt threaten the international trade and payments system. And, of course, there is the tinder of international politics, particularly involving the Middle East, where political and social upheavals can cause major oil disruptions and where fears about and threats to energy supplies can lead to war.[5]

In the mid-1980s, the world experienced an oil glut caused by significantly lower demand for oil by the industrialized nations. A serious recession in the early 1980s in both the USA and Western Europe, the worst in the USA since the Great Depression of the 1930s, led to a reduced demand for oil, a demand that was reduced further by conservation measures, and by the switching to natural gas by some oil consumers. Stimulated by the high oil prices of the 1970s, non-OPEC oil producers increased their production, contributing to a plentiful supply of the resource. The falling oil prices in the mid-1980s caused a number of Western oil companies to close some of their oil wells which were costly to operate and to reduce their budgets for the exploration of new oil. Many analysts now believe that oil prices are likely to start rising again in the late 1980s or the 1990s.

I have focused in this section on the oil crisis, which has affected mainly the industrialized nations. But that is not the full story of the energy crisis which the world faces. About one-half of the world's population uses no fossil fuels at all, relying mainly on wood, charcoal, cow dung, and crop residues for cooking fuel and heat.[6] The shortage of firewood in the Third World is increasing as population growth has caused the consumption of wood to exceed the growth of new supplies in many areas. Forests are being cut down and are not being replanted. The dependency of the poor in the Third World on wood is in some ways like the dependency of the rich on oil. Both dependencies can be dangerous and will require forceful public and private measures to be reduced.

RESPONSES BY GOVERNMENTS TO THE ENERGY CRISIS

Let us look at a few key countries and regions to see how their governments have responded to the energy crisis.

The USA

The American response to the energy crisis has been rather feeble. No coherent policy for dealing with the crisis has been adopted although a number of laws dealing with the crisis have been passed. President Richard Nixon called for "Project Independence" to make the USA self-sufficient in energy by 1980, and President Jimmy Carter believed that the energy crisis should be considered the "moral equivalent of war." But in fact, the US response did not seriously reduce the country's dependency on oil. Why is the USA having difficulty enacting an effective policy to deal with the crisis? Part of the reason is that the inertia of an oil-intensive society is hard to overcome. The nation is used to abundance, in energy as well as in material goods, and the creation of a new outlook and new values is not easy. Also, important groups have conflicting goals relating to energy. The economist Lester Thurow gives the following answer to the question of why the USA has been unable so far to take forceful action to deal with the crisis:

> The lack of action does not spring from a lack of solutions, but from the fact that each solution would cause a large, real income decline for some segment of the population. Everyone is in favor of energy independence in the abstract, but each path to energy independence is vigorously opposed by some significant group that would suffer large income declines if this particular solution were chosen. In the process, all solutions are vetoed and we remain paralyzed. The status quo is painful, but we cannot move.[7]

Some actions have been taken by the US government. Although as yet inadequate to deal with the crisis, some of these responses could have far-reaching importance. Certainly in this last-mentioned category is the decision by the US government, first announced in 1980 during the Carter administration, to use military force if necessary to keep Middle Eastern oil supplies in friendly hands.[8] The creation by the government of a rapid deployment military force is designed to enable the USA to fight in the Middle East on short notice. Arms sales to Saudi Arabia and diplomatic activities are designed to help a pro-Western government maintain control in that key oil-producing country.

The US government's support for nuclear power has been strong. More governmental funds for research and development have been spent on 'this energy source than on any other. Funds designated for the promotion of solar energy increased under the Carter administration in the late 1970s, but the Reagan administration in the early 1980s drastically reduced governmental support for such development. Some laws designed to promote the conservation of energy have been passed, such as the 55 mile per hour speed limit, tax credits for home insulation, and higher fuel efficiency standards for automobiles; but the Reagan administration placed a much lower emphasis on such programs and has budgeted much less money for conservation than did the previous administration. For many years the USA controlled the price of oil and natural gas in the country, partly to protect the profits of American producers. In order to promote the exploration of domestic sources of oil and natural gas and to encourage conservation by higher prices, all controls on oil prices were removed in the early 1980s and a phased reduction of price controls on natural gas was enacted, to be completed by the mid-1980s. In 1980 Congress approved a multi-billion dollar program to develop synthetic fuels, mainly by the converting of large deposits of coal and shale into oil and gas, but in 1985 Congress terminated the program because of falling oil prices and high construction costs. Policies were adopted to encourage electric utilities to shift to using coal instead of oil or natural gas. Finally, a strategic petroleum reserve was established in the mid-1970s, and by the mid-1980s the USA had a four-month supply of oil stored in salt caverns along the Gulf coast.[9]

In summary, one can say that, up through the mid-1980s, US policy emphasized securing and producing more fossil fuels, continuing a strong commitment to nuclear power, promoting and then de-emphasizing solar energy, and promoting energy conservation, first through governmental programs and later by relying on higher prices to decrease use of oil and natural gas.

Western Europe

As mentioned above, many Western European countries are more dependent on imported oil than is the USA. Traditionally, European governments have let the prices for imported fuel go up as the world market determined and have tried to encourage energy conservation through the use of high taxes. France has emphasized nuclear power as its response to the energy crisis, and its plans called for one-half of its electricity to be generated by nuclear power by 1985.[10] West Germany has created a national oil company to explore for oil around the world, and is continuing to construct nuclear power plants, although there is some public opposition to nuclear power; it is also purchasing natural gas from the Soviet Union, and expanding coal production. The discovery of oil under the North Sea has aided mainly Norway and Britain. This large deposit may allow Britain to become self-sufficient in oil, at least for a while. Coal remains a major fuel in Britain, whereas nuclear power has never seriously been developed.

Japan

Japan has no significant oil, natural gas, or coal deposits; as stated above, it is the most vulnerable of all industrialized countries to OPEC's actions. A consensus quickly developed in the country, after the first oil shock in 1973, that its dependency on oil must be reduced. The government encouraged conservation and the people responded. Daniel Yergin reports that "In 1973, Japan used only 57 percent as much energy for every unit of GNP as did the United States. By 1980, it used only 43 percent as much."[11]

It is interesting to note some of the differences between Japanese and American societies that have undoubtedly affected their different responses to the energy crisis. Because of their history and their limited land and resources, Japanese society has always assumed scarcity and insecurity of resources such as fuel, whereas American society is used to abundance and has assumed it would continue. Japanese industries have been traditionally more willing than their American counterparts to make long-term investments, the American companies often being more concerned with making short-term profits. The Japanese know that their goods must compete well in international trade if they are to maintain their high living standards. Japan is used to change and adaptation. The consensus that developed in Japan after 1973 emphasized a shift from consumption to constraint. It included a belief that the economy had to shift to "knowledge-intensive" industries which use relatively little energy, and that energy efficiency was the key element in the adjustment the country needed to make to this new situation.[12] The Japanese government also has a billion-dollar research program, called Operation Sunshine, designed to make the Japanese the leaders in solar energy technology. Partly because of strong public opposition to nuclear power – mainly derived from the experiences of the atomic bombing of Hiroshima and Nagasaki – nuclear power has been developed only on a small scale in the country.

China

China's energy crisis is a typical one for a Third World country: how to provide enough fuel for a rapidly expanding population. The Chinese government estimates that, of the 800 million people living in rural areas, 500 million experience a serious shortage of fuel for three to five months of every year, and in the worst-off provinces about 70 percent of the people are short of fuel for up to one half of every year.[13] The situation is so bad, according to one report, that in rural areas,

> every available source which can conceivably burn [is burned]; stumps and tree roots are dug out; branches are lopped away; bark stripped from living trees; leaves, fallen twigs and other debris are raked; grasses are cut; pieces of sod are carved out; dry animal dung is collected. And when all other possibilities vanish, peasants grow sweet potatoes on any odd patch of land and use dried tubers for fuel.[14]

According to the above-cited report, in spite of governmental efforts to plant trees, "deforestation, traditionally associated with the dissipation and neglect of pre-Communist China, has actually spread and accelerated at unprecedented rates since 1949."[15] The private planting of trees for firewood is prohibited for ideological reasons: it is equated with promoting capitalism. The author of this report, a Canadian geographer, believes that the main causes of the deforestation are the longstanding "grains first" policy, which emphasized growing food crops, and excessive lumbering and fuel gathering.[16]

China has the world's largest program to create methane gas for use as fuel in rural areas. The gas is produced by fermenting animal and human wastes in simple generators; after the gas is produced, a rich organic fertilizer remains which can safely be used on crops.[17]

The Chinese use relatively little oil, given the size of China's population, and the country is able to export 10 percent of its output. According to a report from a study of energy and security at Harvard University, "The Chinese do not need to be told to conserve energy – they already do. In the winter, there is virtually no heat anywhere, except in hotels frequented by foreigners. Concert halls and opera houses, universities, and even trains are unheated."[18] The Harvard study concluded that, assuming that the Chinese energy-conserving behavior does not change as it continues to industrialize, "the Chinese appear relatively immune to the threat of any production disruption in the Middle East."[19] The Chinese production of oil may also increase dramatically in the coming decade, since offshore drilling by foreign oil companies has begun in areas which have potentially large reserves of oil.

THE EFFECT OF THE ENERGY CRISIS ON THIRD WORLD DEVELOPMENT PLANS

The early stages of industrialization are energy-intensive. Modern transportation systems, upon which industrialization rests, utilize large amounts of energy, as does the construction industry. The huge increase in oil prices in the 1970s cast a cloud over the development plans of many developing nations. Most of these plans were based upon an assumption that reasonably cheap oil would be available, as it had been for the West, to support their industrialization. Most of the Third World countries have little or no coal or oil themselves. The development plans called for these countries to export natural commodities, non-fuel resources, and light manufactured goods; it was assumed that the earnings from these exports would be sufficient to pay for the fuel they would need to import. The success of the development plans also depended upon the countries being able to generate enough capital locally so that funds for investment in businesses would be available.

When OPEC increased fuel prices, no exceptions were made for the poorer countries; they were required to pay the same high prices for their oil imports as the rich nations had to pay. Added to this burden was the one created by the global recession which the higher oil prices had helped to create. As the recession deepened in the West, the industrialized countries cut back on their imports from the developing nations. Many of these countries borrowed heavily from commercial banks to pay for their higher oil bills and accumulated staggering debts. The World Bank estimates the foreign debt of the less developed countries in the mid-1980s to be $900 billion.[20] Brazil had the largest foreign debt of all the developing nations, about $100 billion in 1985, and was having serious troubles in trying to repay it.[21]

The new situation created by high oil prices has led some experts to talk about a "Fourth World." This term refers to some of the developing nations, such as Bangladesh, which have few natural resources of their own and little ability to purchase the now expensive oil to promote industrialization. The countries in the Fourth World, the "poor poor," have little chance of ever developing along the path followed by the West with its dependency on fossil fuels. If these nations are to improve their living standards, they will have to follow a development path radically different from the one followed by the developed nations.

Many energy experts believe that there is little hope that conservation can help very much to improve the energy crisis in the Third World since there is little waste of energy there now. And many experts predict that the largest increase in demand for oil for the remaining part of this century will come from the industrializing Third World nations with high population growth, and not from the developed nations, which have low population growth and are becoming more energy-efficient.[22]

Population pressure and the high cost of oil are putting increased strain on the traditional fuel in the Third World, which is mainly wood. This problem has been mentioned above and will be discussed further in chapter 5 on the environment. As firewood becomes expensive or unavailable in rural areas, people switch to burning dried cow dung and crop residues, thus preventing important nutrients and organic material from returning to the soil.

THE RELATIONSHIP BETWEEN ENERGY USE AND DEVELOPMENT

A Shift in Types of Energy

One way to study the progress of the human race is to focus on the way humans have used energy to help them produce goods and services. People have constantly sought ways to lighten the physical work they must do to produce the things that they need – or feel they need – to live decently. The harnessing of fire was a crucial step in human evolution as it provided early humans with heat, enabled them to cook their foods, and helped them to protect themselves against carnivorous animals. Next came the domestication of animals. Animal power was an important supplement to human muscles, enabling people to grow food on a larger scale than ever before. Wood was the most important energy source for much of human history, and it still is for a large part of the world's population. The replacement of wood by coal to make steam in Britain in the eighteenth century enabled the Industrial Revolution to begin. In the late 1800s oil, and in the early 1900s natural gas, began to replace coal since they were cleaner and more convenient to use. As figure 8 shows, oil had overtaken coal as the principal commercial energy source in the world by 1970. In the 1970s nuclear power was introduced, but, as can be seen in figure 8, this was still a minor source of energy in 1980.

Increased Use

As figure 8 clearly shows, the use of energy in the world has increased dramatically in the years since the end of World War II, a period of rapid development in the industrialized countries and one

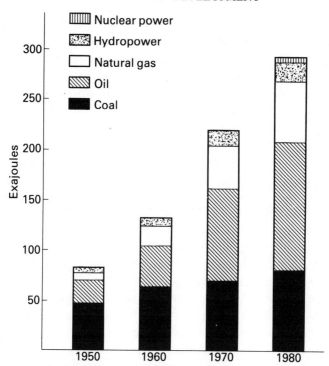

Figure 8 World commercial energy use, by source.

Source: United Nations, *World Energy Supplies*; presented in Daniel Deudney and Christopher Flavin, *Renewable Energy* (New York: W. W. Norton, 1983), p. 11. Reprinted by permission. Copyright © Worldwatch Institute 1983.

marking the beginning of industrialization in a number of Third World countries. Up to 1980, most of the increased energy use took place in the developed nations. The USA was the largest user of energy from 1950 to 1980: in 1980 the USA, with about 5 percent of the world's population, was using about one-third of the energy being used by all nations. The USA consumes more energy annually than does all of Western Europe, even though the population of the latter exceeds that of the former by 75 percent.[23] While the energy use per person in the USA exceeded that of other developed nations in 1980, the difference between the energy use of the USA and that of the developing nations was so great as to be hard to comprehend. Per capita energy consumption for commercial activity in India in 1980 was about 400 pounds of coal equivalent of energy, while in the USA it was about 23,000 pounds. In Bangladesh it was only about 100 pounds.[24]

Americans use a lot of their energy for transportation, and that means automobiles, and more recently trucks.[25] The Americans are the most mobile people in the history of the world. They are the world's modern nomads; but instead of using camels or horses as other nomads do, they use the car. An examination of what has happened to cars in the USA shows one reason why American energy use increased dramatically in the 1950s, 1960s, and early 1970s. Let's look at what happened to one model of an American car – the Ford Thunderbird. Table 7 shows that the length, weight, and engine size of Thunderbirds increased from 1955 to 1975. The price of gasoline was low and stable during most of the years when the model was getting bigger, heavier, and more powerful.[26] After there was a large increase in the price of gasoline, the car became smaller, lighter, and less powerful in 1980.

One can't fully explain the increased use of energy in the USA in the 1950s, 1960s, and early 1970s by focusing on what was happening to just one model of an American car, of course, but such a focus does help us to understand an important part of the story. Heavier and more powerful cars use significantly more fuel than lighter and less powerful ones, and the trend in American cars in the decades before the oil shocks was in the direction of more weight and greater power. And the key role played by the

Table 7 The evolution of an American automobile:
the Ford Thunderbird

	Length	weight (lb)	Engine size (displacement in in³)	Leaded gasoline ($ per gal.)
1955	14'7"	3,300	290	0.29
1960	17'1"	4,300	350	0.31
1965	17'1"	4,600	390	0.31
1970	17'8"	4,600	430	0.36
1975	18'10"	5,100	460	0.57
1980	16'8"	3,200	260	1.23

Source: Adapted from *The New York Times*, city edn (July 21, 1980), p. A12.

automobile in the US economy is illustrated by the fact that, in the mid-1970s, nine of the ten largest companies in the world, six of which were American, sold either oil or cars.[27]

Recession and Higher Prices Reduce Demand for Oil

As we have seen, after the first oil shock in 1973, most Americans returned to their old ways of high consumption of oil and other forms of energy. The panic which came with the oil embargo, and which led to a high demand for smaller, more fuel-efficient autos, soon passed once the embargo was lifted and gasoline supplies were plentiful again. Even though gasoline prices were higher after the embargo, they were not high enough to discourage people from buying large cars. But when the second oil shock hit the West in 1979–80, coming as it did during a recession, many Americans came to the conclusion that the energy crisis was real, and there was then a dramatic shift in the USA to purchasing small automobiles and driving less. Many turned to buying cars imported from Japan, which were recognized as being well made and much more fuel-efficient than most American models. The rush to buy imports caused a crisis in the US automobile industry since there was no longer a large market for its big cars. The industry has always preferred selling larger cars to smaller ones because profits are higher on the larger models. But after much agony, the near-collapse of one of the large auto companies (Chrysler), and a large financial investment, the American companies shifted to producing smaller cars with good fuel-efficiency ratings. In the mid-1980s, however, many Americans were again showing a preference for larger automobiles because of the oil glut and lower gasoline prices.[28]

The Decoupling of Energy Consumption and Economic Growth

Historically, there has appeared to be a one-to-one relationship in the USA between economic growth and energy growth; for example, a 10 percent increase in the amount of goods and services produced in the country was accompanied by an approximately 10 percent increase in the amount of energy consumed. But the oil shock of 1973 seems to have broken this relationship. In 1981 the

industrial world consumed only about 5 percent more energy than
it had in 1973 even though it had a real GNP growth of over 20
percent; in other words, the developed countries were using about
15 percent less energy in 1981 than they would have under the
one-to-one relationship between energy use and economic
growth.[29] What happened was that the developed nations had
begun to use their energy much more efficiently than they had
before 1973, no doubt in response to the higher oil prices.

This partial decoupling between energy use and economic
growth is not surprising once one realizes that there are a number of
countries with high levels of economic prosperity which have
traditionally used much less energy than does the USA. Sweden, a
country with a higher living standard than the USA and higher
heating requirements, uses about one-half of the energy per person
that the USA uses; West Germany, another wealthy country which
has had impressive economic growth, also uses about one-half of
the energy the USA uses per capita. A number of studies of the US
energy situation have concluded that a more efficient use of energy
in the USA can actually lead to economic growth.[30] A study
prepared for the US President, recommending actions the country
should take to deal with the situation presented in the government's
Global 2000 Report, describes some of the energy inefficiencies in
the US economy:

> Evidence is mounting that US economic growth, as measured
> by Gross National Product (GNP), need not be tied to a
> similar energy growth rate. The most important reason is that
> the US economy, including much of its building and
> transportation stock, its industrial processes and machinery, is
> inefficient in its use of energy, compared both with other
> economies and with the technological and cost-effective
> options that already exist. The opportunity is enormous for
> improving the energy efficiency of US capital stock – in effect,
> creating "conservation energy" – to get the same desirable end
> result of warmth, comfort, jobs, and mobility that fossil fuel
> energy provides.[31]

Energy conservation can promote economic growth because the
cost of saving energy through such measures as improving the fuel

efficiency of cars, improving the efficiency of industrial processes, insulating houses, etc., is lower than the cost of most energy today. Also, investments in improving the energy efficiency of American autos, homes, and factories create many new jobs and businesses throughout the country, thus spurring the growth of the economy in contrast to draining funds out of the economy by purchasing foreign oil.

Part of the reason many European countries use much less energy per person than the USA is that they are smaller countries with populations not nearly as dispersed. One study has shown that the long distances people and goods move in the USA, in contrast with Europe and Japan, and the American preference for large, single-family homes, accounts for about 40 percent of the difference between high US energy use and lower foreign use. The other 60 percent of the difference is accounted for by the fact that the fuel economy of American automobiles has historically been much poorer than that of many foreign cars and the energy consumption per unit of output of many American manufacturing firms is higher than that of the foreign companies.[32]

The USA cannot obviously do anything about its size, but there are things that can be done to improve the energy efficiency of its transportation equipment. As mentioned above, the federal government passed a law in 1975, over the strong opposition of the automobile industry, requiring the fuel efficiency of American automobiles to be gradually improved.[33] About 90 percent of the long-distance hauling of freight in the USA is by truck,[34] and a truck uses four times as much energy to move a ton of freight as does a freight train.[35] The US government, by its vast expenditure of funds on the interstate highway system (reported to be the largest public works project in history), its much lower tax on gasoline than in Europe, and its relatively small amount of expenditures that benefit the railroads, has done much to promote the use of trucks over trains in the country. This policy could be reversed.

THE GREENHOUSE EFFECT

Some scientists believe that the human race is now involved in an experiment of unprecedented importance to the future of life on this planet, involving nothing less than the global climate. A change in the global climate may now be taking place, mainly because of the burning, by humans, of large amounts of fossil fuels – coal, oil, and natural gas. When these fuels are consumed, carbon, which accumulated in them over millions of years, is released into the atmosphere as a gas, carbon dioxide (CO_2). Scientists are in general agreement that CO_2 in the earth's atmosphere has increased significantly since the Industrial Revolution: by about 15–25 percent between 1800 and 1980.[36] This increase, according to some scientists, will cause a warming of the earth's surface – the "greenhouse effect" – since CO_2 in the atmosphere allows sunlight to reach the earth, but traps some of the earth's heat, preventing it from radiating back into space.[37]

There is no controversy over the increase in CO_2 levels in the earth's atmosphere, but there is controversy among scientists as to whether the increasing CO_2 will actually cause a warming of the earth. So far there has been no clear indication that the earth's temperature is rising.[38] But the supporters of the greenhouse effect theory believe that temporary climatic changes may be masking the longer-term warming change which is going on and that by the end of the present century the warming trend will make itself clear.[39]

A doubling of the amount of carbon dioxide in the atmosphere could lead to significant changes in the earth's climate. This will probably take place in the middle of the next century, if the rate of consumption of fossil fuels equals that which took place during much of the 1970s.[40] It is estimated that a doubling of the CO_2 level could lead to an average global warming of about 5 degrees Fahrenheit.[41] While 5 degrees doesn't sound like very much, it would be a significant change. According to scientists of the US National Aeronautics and Space Administration, the temperature on earth "would approach the warmth of the Mesozoic, the age of dinosaurs."[42] There would be major changes in the amount of rainfall and its location, with some areas getting more rainfall than at present and some less. Parts of the world will have a better climate for growing food and parts will have worse. Scientists are unable to predict reliably which areas would be hurt and which would gain, but there is speculation that some of the major food-growing regions of the world at present, such as the central and western USA would be seriously harmed by the climatic changes. It is estimated that much of the USA would have hot, dry conditions, and that the "corn belt" would move north and into an area which does not have such fertile land. India, the Middle East, and sections of Africa could have better climate for agriculture than they have now.[43]

Another possible effect of a warming of the earth's climate is that the level of the oceans might rise, by as much as 15–25 feet, especially if the West Antarctic ice sheet melts. Such a rising of waters, which could take place over several decades, could lead to the gradual evacuation of many coastal cities around the world. A rise of the sea level of approximately 15 feet would flood about 25 percent of Louisiana and Florida, 10 percent of New Jersey, and many other lowlands around the world.[44]

The world faces a real dilemma concerning this situation. A report by the US Council on Environmental Quality, which examines many of the relevant scientific studies on the CO_2 problem, explains the predicament:

> The carbon dioxide problem poses an extraordinarily difficult dilemma for the international community of nations. To respond in a significant way now to a threat whose scope and time of onset are still uncertain might require unnecessary commitments of resources. To postpone taking action until a substantial climate change were detected – which could be 20 years away – would entail a risk of being unable to prevent long-term climate changes that could prove serious and irreversible for centuries.[45]

There *are* energy policies that the USA and other nations could pursue which would alleviate this threat but would not require them to make a serious sacrifice at present. One would be to de-emphasize programs to promote the increased use of coal and synthetic fuels made from coal and oil and to stress the conservation of energy and the development of renewable energy sources, such as solar energy, and non-fossil fuel energy, such as nuclear energy. Another policy would be to combat deforestation, since trees, along with other vegetation, absorb large amounts of carbon dioxide.[46] (The increasing destruction of the great tropical rain forests in Latin America is seen by some experts as representing a real threat to the global climate.) The United Nations is coordinating scientific research efforts directed at this problem, but, as the US government report cited above states, the world probably cannot afford to wait until the evidence is clear. The view of Gus Speth, the former Chairman of the Council on Environmental Quality, is that,

> With our limited knowledge of its [the earth's] workings, we should not experiment with its great systems in a way that imposes unknown and potentially large risks on future generations . . . People have altered the face of the planet throughout history, but the power of today's technology and our growing capacity to foresee, however uncertainly, the possible consequences of our acts puts us in a new moral position.[47]

THE ENERGY TRANSITION

The world is entering a period of transition from one main energy source – oil – to a new principal source or a variety of sources. This is the third energy transition the world has passed through: the first was from wood to coal, and the second from coal to oil. Many people, although not all by any means, now recognize that the industrialized world must shift from its reliance on depletable, nonrenewable fossil fuels to an energy source or sources which are renewable or, for all practical purposes, non-depletable. Many in the USA and in the other non-communist industrialized countries understand that their dependence on imported oil must end since it is no longer cheap, abundant, or secure. But what will be the new principal energy source for the industries of the developed world and for those of the developing nations? As in many periods of transition, this is not yet clear. The only clear thing now is that the old state of affairs is no longer viable.

Since we are only at the beginning of the energy transition, a period which will no doubt take many years to pass through, it is interesting to note what the first response by the largest energy consumers in the world was to the need to develop new energy sources. In figure 9 we see that in the early 1980s the overwhelming amount of funds for research and development was going to nonrenewable energy sources (nuclear energy and fossil fuels); the sum of expenditures by governments and industry on renewable energy sources and on conservation was minor in comparison.

For the rest of this section, we shall examine some of the potentialities of the most often discussed energy sources, and in the final section we shall focus on nuclear energy, looking in some detail at the main arguments of its supporters and its critics. Energy sources can be divided into those which are nonrenewable (that is, they are being used up) and those that are renewable, in the sense that most of them gain their energy from the sun, which is expected to continue to shine at its present brightness for several billion more years.

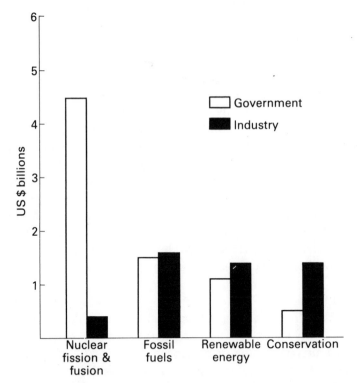

Figure 9 Government and industry energy research and development expenditures in 17 industrialized countries, 1981.

Source: International Energy Agency; presented in Daniel Deudney and Christopher Flavin, *Renewable Energy* (New York: W. W. Norton, 1983), p. 263. Reprinted by permission. Copyright © Worldwatch Institute 1983.

Nonrenewable Energy Sources

Oil, natural gas, coal, and uranium are the main sources of non-renewable energy. A four-year study of the energy situation which was published by the National Academy of Sciences predicts that world oil production will peak in the 1990s and gradually decline thereafter.[48] The production of both oil and natural gas in the USA peaked around 1970.[49]

Coal is a much more abundant resource than oil or natural gas, and the USA has very large deposits of it, as do the Soviet Union, China, and Europe. Although the switch back to coal in the USA has not been as fast or as strong as many predicted, many energy analysts expect that this fuel will play a prominent role in the transition period. But the use of coal presents many problems, some of which resulted in the switch to oil after World War II. I was reminded of one of coal's main disadvantages – its polluting effect – when I took my young son to see an old coal-burning passenger train make an excursion run through our town a short time ago. The black clouds of smoke from the locomotive brought back memories from my childhood when trains like this one passed through our town regularly. Those black clouds dramatized one of the great improvements which came with the arrival of the relatively clean diesel oil trains. While improvements in technology, such as the use of expensive "scrubbers" on electric generating plants which burn coal, can remove many of the dangerous pollutants caused by burning coal, others remain. And no affordable technology can prevent the build-up of carbon dioxide in the atmosphere which comes from burning coal and other fossil fuels.

In addition, over half of the coal in the USA is west of the Mississippi River, in deposits relatively close to the surface. The preferred way of extracting such deposits is by strip mining, a process which wreaks havoc on the land. Efforts to reclaim the land afterwards are very expensive and very imperfect. The coal that lies in the eastern part of the country can be obtained only by underground mining, a process that is known to be inherently dangerous, unhealthy, and filled with labor–management conflict.

The making of synthetic oil and gas from coal and oil shale has been considered by some as the way to make the USA less dependent on foreign oil. A multi-billion-dollar effort to develop energy this way was approved by Congress in 1980. Vast oil shale deposits lie in Colorado and Wyoming, but the processing of oil shale relies on strip mining and requires vast amounts of water, which is scarce in the West. Efforts to develop this potential source of energy collapsed in the mid-1980s as several large American oil companies withdrew from these ventures because of high construction costs, high interest rates, lowered demand for energy throughout the country, and falling imported oil prices. The US government ended all of its financing for synthetic fuel projects in 1985. Canada has large deposits of tar sands from which oil can be extracted. But in the mid-1980s Canada too was experiencing serious difficulties developing these deposits as several major oil companies withdrew from the development, leaving the Canadian government the sole developer in some cases.

It is possible that uranium, the basic fuel for nuclear energy, is widely distributed around the world, but the bulk of positively identified deposits are located in a relatively few countries, one of which is the USA. The mining of uranium can, and has, led to cancer, and the waste products from the mining are radioactive. The USA has fairly abundant supplies of uranium, but, like coal, they will eventually run out.

Renewable Energy Sources

The energy from the sun can be obtained in a variety of ways: from wood, falling water, wind, wastes, and direct sunlight. We will briefly examine each of these.

First, wood is still the principal fuel for nearly one-third of humanity.[50] Rapidly expanding populations in the Third World are placing high demands on the use of wood; at the same time, modern agricultural requirements and development in general are leading to the clearing of vast acres of forests. Acute shortages of firewood already exist in wide areas of Africa, Asia, and Latin America. The US Government's *Global 2000 Report* projects that the demand for wood for fuel will exceed supplies by about 25 percent before the year 2000.[51]

Second, hydroelectric power, which is generated from falling water, is a clean source of energy, causing little pollution. A large potential for developing this type of energy still exists in Africa, Latin America, and Asia, although many of the rivers which could be used are located far from the centers of population. Large dams, which are often necessary to store the water for the electric generators, usually seriously disturb the local environment, and there is still no known way to prevent the silting behind the dam which limits its life. While most of the best sites for large dams in the industrialized countries have already been developed, a potential exists for constructing some small dams and for installing electric generators at existing dams which do not have them.

Third, wind is an energy source which was commonly used in the past for power as well as for the cooling of houses. It is still used for these purposes in some Third World countries and has recently gained new respect in the USA, especially in California, where wind turbines have been constructed in areas which have fairly steady wind. A potential exists for the wider exploitation of this source of energy, and modern technology is producing more efficient wind collectors. The main problem with wind, of course, is that it is usually not steady, and thus the energy it creates must be stored in some way so it can be used when the wind dies down. There is not yet any easy and inexpensive way to do this. Another problem with wind is that the choice windy places in the world are relatively few, unevenly distributed, and often not near population centers.

Fourth, biomass conversion is the name given to the production of liquid and gaseous fuel from crop, animal, and human wastes; from garbage from cities; and from crops especially grown for energy production. Millions of generators which create methane gas from animal and human wastes are producing fuel for villages in India and China. Brazil is using the residues from its large sugar-cane production to produce alcohol for fuel for automobiles and is experimenting with growing cassava, a common root crop, for conversion into alcohol. St Louis and some other US cities are burning their garbage mixed with coal and/or natural gas to produce electricity. It is difficult to estimate how widespread this form of energy generation will become in the future. Some see good potential while others mention its negative aspects, such as the emission of harmful gases and foul odors from burning garbage, and the use of land to grow energy crops instead of food crops in a hungry world.

Fifth, the use of direct sunlight probably has the greatest potential of all the forms of solar energy for becoming a major source of energy in the future. Direct sunlight can be used to heat space and water, or to produce electricity by using the photovoltaic or solar cell. The solar cell, which is usually made from silicon, was developed for use in the US space exploration program, and extensive research is now being carried on to adapt it for private use.[52] It is still expensive, however, and its high cost is probably the most serious hindrance to its wider use. A major reduction in its cost would probably come about if it were mass-produced, but without a large demand for solar cells, which their high cost prevents, mass production facilities will not be built by private enterprise. A way out of the vicious cycle could come through large purchases by the government, which one of solar energy's strong supporters – Barry Commoner – has advocated;[53] or it could come as the cost of other types of energy continue to rise. Solar cells could be used well in moderately or intensely sunny places. Much of the Third World fits this criterion. The Third World is, in fact, often mentioned as a vast potential market for solar cells because many of its rural areas still lack electricity, and solar energy is collected about as efficiently by small, decentralized collectors as it is by larger, centralized units.

Finally, geothermal energy – heat that is produced within the earth's interior and stored often in pools of water, in rock, or as steam under the earth's cool crust – is not a form of solar energy but it is a renewable form of energy. Iceland uses this form of energy to heat many of its homes, and the Soviet Union and Hungary heat extensive greenhouses with it. Two US cities, one in Oregon and one in Idaho, use geothermal energy, and a geothermal power plant which produces electricity has been built in northern California. For a few favorable locations in the world, geothermal energy can be utilized, but it is not expected to have a wider potential.

Conservation

Conservation is not commonly thought of as an energy source, but according to a study of the US energy situation by the Harvard Business School, it should properly be regarded as a major untapped source of energy. The Harvard study concludes that conservation, rather than coal or nuclear energy, is the major alternative to imported oil.[54] How much energy could the USA save by adopting conservation measures? The Harvard study found that the savings could be impressive:

> If the United States were to make a serious commitment to conservation, it might well consume 30 to 40 percent less energy than it now does, and still enjoy the same or an even higher standard of living. That saving would not hinge on a major technological breakthrough, and it would require only modest adjustments in the way people live.[55]

To many people, the term "conservation" means deprivation, a doing without something; but the Harvard study, and many others, have shown that much energy conservation can take place in the USA without causing any real hardship. There are three ways in which one can save energy: by performing some activity in a more energy-efficient manner; by using energy that is currently being wasted; and by changing one's behavior to reduce the use of energy.

Many American businesses now recognize that making their operations more energy-efficient is a good way to increase their profits. The investments they make to improve their business operations and reduce their energy usage are soon repaid by their reduced energy bills. One of the most impressive examples is IBM, which set out in 1973 to reduce its energy use by 10 percent and ended up reducing it by 45 percent.[56] Dow Chemical Company discovered after the 1973 oil crisis that its standard practice up to then was never to turn off its de-icing equipment during the year, so that its sidewalks and service areas were being warmed even on the Fourth of July. American industry has made impressive gains in reducing its energy consumption, but much still can be done, since American industry – and American society as a whole – is accustomed to many wasteful practices adopted before 1973 when energy was cheap.

One major conservation method US industry could adopt is called "cogeneration," which is the combined production of both electricity and heat in the same installation. Electricity is currently produced by private and public utilities, and the heat from the generation of the electricity is passed off into the air or into lakes and rivers as waste. With cogeneration plants, the heat from the production of electricity – often in the form of steam – is used for industrial processes or for heating homes and offices. The production of electricity and steam together uses about one-half the amount of fuel as does their production separately.[57] Cogeneration is fairly common in Europe, but not in the USA, where electric utilities oppose this form of competition, and often give cheaper rates to their big industrial customers, thus reducing their incentive to adopt the process.

If the USA ever does reach the goal of energy savings which the Harvard report believes is possible, it will be because of a combination of governmental policies which encourage conservation and action by millions of individuals. The USA is a country where people respond well to incentives, but so far national governmental incentives to promote conservation practices have been rather weak. For several years the federal government allowed a person who insulated his or her home or installed a solar water heater to deduct 15 percent of the cost of the energy improvement from his or her income tax. The state of California allows a person to deduct 55 percent of the cost of solar devices from his or her state tax. (This law no doubt partly explains why California leads the nation in the number of solar devices installed in its homes.) The city of Davis, California, has changed its building code so that all new homes in the city must meet certain energy performance standards. American homes are notorious wasters of energy. In sunny South Carolina houses with black roofs are common, although it is a long-established fact that a light-colored roof reflects some of the hot summer sun. Houses and apartments with large window surfaces facing the south can gain much heat from the low winter sun, and these windows can be shaded by trees or an overhang to keep out the high summer sun. The popular all-glass American skyscrapers built during the 1960s are huge energy wasters, since their large areas of glass absorb the hot summer rays. Since their windows cannot be opened, at times the buildings' air conditioners must work at peak levels just to cool their interiors to the same temperature as the outside air. Simple measures like planting trees to obtain shade can have a significant cooling effect on a house, a city street, or a parking lot – reducing temperatures by as much as 10–20 degrees over unshaded areas. Town houses, the modern name for the old row houses, are again becoming popular in many cities; these are much more energy-efficient than the common, single-family house because of their shared walls. According to a study by the American Institute of Architects, "improved design of new buildings and modification of old ones could save a third of our current total energy use – and save money too."[58]

Let me end this section with a short story about a personal blunder which illustrates several conservation principles. A short while ago my hot water heater stopped working. I was greatly relieved when the plumber assured me that he could replace it right away so we could soon have hot water. I remembered that the government had a policy of rating appliances for their energy efficiency, and asked the plumber if the water heater he would install was energy-efficient. "Oh yes," he replied, "it has a sticker on it." I was also pleased to hear that the price of the heater would be lower than I feared it might be. After the new heater was installed, I read the label on it which rated its use of energy and found to my dismay, and embarrassment, that the heater had the lowest rating that was possible to give on that model. A water heater lasts about 15 years, so I will have to pay for my error for some time. (An insulation blanket wrapped around the water heater later helped to reduce the heater's deficiencies.)

In addition to teaching me that conservation requires careful planning, this little episode illustrated well to me a key aspect of energy conservation and explained why many people don't do it. Conservation often requires an initial investment – the more efficient water heaters are more expensive than the least efficient – and the decision to spend more now in order to save in the future is not always easy to make. People naturally look at the purchase price of the appliance – or home – and often follow the rule, "the cheaper the better," as long as the appliance or home is adequate. What that price does not tell you, but what the government's sticker on my water heater did tell, is how much it will cost to run that appliance, or heat and air-condition that home, over the years you use it.

Knowing that saving energy often takes an initial investment helps one understand why the decontrol of prices of oil and natural gas, which will lead to higher prices of those fuels, is probably not enough by itself to cause many people to use less energy. The better educated and more affluent might recognize that an investment in insulation or a more expensive water heater makes good sense and will save them money over the long run, but those with lower incomes do not have the extra money to make the initial investment. Some of the poor spend a higher portion of their income on energy than do those on higher incomes, and thus could benefit greatly from the better-insulated house or the more fuel-efficient car, but they usually end up with a poorly insulated house and a gas-guzzling car. Higher prices for fuel will probably help to reduce energy consumption, but stronger governmental incentives and regulations, such as substantially higher tax credits for installing insulation and substantially higher fuel efficiency standards for automobiles, could produce a significant movement toward conservation.

NUCLEAR POWER: A CASE STUDY

In this final section we shall look closely at nuclear power, which is surrounded by political controversy. The supporters and critics of nuclear power are currently locked in a battle which could decide the fate of this form of energy. Before we examine the main arguments which each side presents, we will first look at a brief history of the development of nuclear power so that we can better understand the arguments each side makes.

The Potential and the Peril

Nuclear power was seen by many in its early years as the answer to the world's energy needs. Its promoters claimed it would be a non-polluting and safe form of energy which could produce electricity "too cheap to meter." After the destructive power of the atom was demonstrated with the bombing of Hiroshima and Nagasaki, people welcomed the thought that atomic research could also be used for peaceful purposes. The first prototype of a commercial nuclear power plant began operation in the USA in 1957. Figure 10 shows the growth of nuclear research and power reactors in the world from 1942 to 1981 and the increasing number of countries which have acquired these reactors. More and more countries have shown a desire to acquire knowledge about nuclear energy.

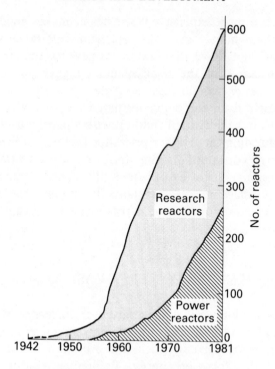

No. of countries possessing reactors

Figure 10 The world's nuclear industry.

Source: John Holdren, "Nuclear Power and Nuclear Weapons: The Connection is Dangerous," *Bulletin of the Atomic Scientists*, 39 (January 1983), p. 40. Reprinted by permission.

The first generation of nuclear power reactors are known as fission, light-water reactors. They utilize the same process which was used to explode the early atomic bombs – the splitting of the core (the nucleus) of the atoms of heavy elements, which releases tremendous energy. Uranium 235 (U-235) is the fuel used in these reactors. The chain-reaction which comes with the splitting of the uranium nucleus is controlled in the power reactors to produce sustained heat, which is then used, as it is in coal- and oil-fed power plants, to produce steam. The steam drives the turbines that generate electricity.

The uranium which is used in the common light-water reactors must be enriched so that it contains a higher percentage of U-235 than is found in nature. This is done in very large, very expensive, enrichment plants that utilize huge amounts of electricity themselves. Because of the difficulty of obtaining the required U-235, it was originally planned to reprocess the spent fuel rods from the power reactors to extract unused uranium, thus making uranium supplies last longer. Controversy has surrounded these reprocessing plants, partly because plutonium, one of the deadliest known substances and the fuel for the Nagasaki bomb (the bomb dropped on Hiroshima utilized uranium), is produced during the reprocessing. Three commercial reprocessing plants were built in the USA – one in Illinois, one in New York, and one in South Carolina – but none is operating at present. The shutdowns occurred because of technical difficulties, safety concerns, and the fear that such plants made plutonium too accessible.

Another way to handle the relative scarcity of fuel for the light-water reactors would be by building a second generation of power reactors. These reactors, known as the fast-breeder reactors, use plutonium as their fuel and will actually produce more fuel than they consume. The attractiveness of this feature was countered by the great complexity of the plants and the increased danger which would come from an accident, since plutonium was being used instead of the less radioactive uranium. Plutonium is extremely harmful if inhaled or digested, and it has a half-life (the amount of time for one-half of the substance to disintegrate or be transformed into something else) of over 24,000 years. The Soviet Union began operating a fast-breeder reactor in the early 1970s, and India completed constructing an experimental breeder reactor in the mid-1980s. After spending nearly $2 billion on an effort to build a demonstration breeder reactor, the US government abandoned the effort in 1983 because of technical difficulties, safety concerns, and spiraling costs. In 1984 five European countries (Britain, France, West Germany, Belgium, and Italy) agreed to pool their efforts to build breeder reactors.

Fusion nuclear power, which is still in the experimental stage, might be called a third generation of nuclear energy. Fusion energy is created by the same process that creates the energy in the sun and is the process used in the hydrogen or H-bomb, which is vastly more powerful than the fission atomic bombs. Instead of splitting atoms, as happens in fission, in fusion atoms are fused together. The process is highly complicated and demands temperatures (millions of degrees) and pressures with which scientists have little experience. The attractiveness of the process is that much of its fuel (deuterium) comes from seawater and is non-radioactive, while the other main component of its fuel (tritium), which is radioactive, can be obtained from a substance (lithium) which is fairly abundant.[59] Much less radioactive waste would come from the fusion process than from the fission process and it is an inherently safer process than fission. Recent experiments, some of the main ones conducted in the US at Princeton University, have demonstrated the feasibility of the fusion process.[60] Even if experiments in fusion continue to be successful, a practical demonstration of the process is not expected before the year 2000, and any widespread use of this form of energy will probably not come until well into the twenty-first century.

Nuclear power is in serious difficulty around the world, with only France and the Soviet Union aggressively promoting it. It is expected that Japan will proceed with plans to expand its nuclear energy plants, but in many Western European countries there has been little new construction and few orders for new plants. In the USA there have been no new orders for nuclear power plants since 1977, and about 100 orders for plants were cancelled during the 1970s.[61] The slowdown in nuclear power growth in the USA has occurred because of the reduced demand for electricity (caused by the rapidly increasing cost of power, conservation measures, and an economic recession), the skyrocketing cost of building the plants (plants that were originally estimated to cost $200–$300 million now cost $1–$2 billion), and increasing concern for the safety of the plants.

In 1979 a major accident – a near melt-down of the uranium fuel – occurred in a nuclear power plant at Three Mile Island, Pennsylvania, leading to a release of some radioactive steam and gas from the plant and the consequent official recommendation that nearby pregnant women as well as young children be evacuated.

Although no one was killed in this accident, and the release of the radioactive substances was later judged by a presidential investigation committee to have caused no danger to public health,[62] the clean-up from the accident will cost about $1 billion,[63] and the accident increased public fears about nuclear power. It has been estimated that new safety requirements for nuclear power plants which were issued by the federal government after Three Mile Island, as well as delays in construction of new plants and more temporary shutdowns of existing plants caused by the concerns raised by the Three Mile Island accident, will add $130 billion to the cost of nuclear electricity in the USA between 1979 and 1992.[64]

In 1986 a nuclear power plant at Chernobyl in the Soviet Union exploded. More than 100,000 people were evacuated from an area of about 300 square miles around the plant. The accident spread radiation around the world with some European countries receiving significant amounts of it. About 30 people died from the catastrophe during the following few months, and a Soviet government report made a rough estimate that up to 45,000 extra cancer deaths might be possible in the Soviet Union because of the incident.[65] It is believed that both flaws in the design of the reactor and mistakes by the operators of the plant were responsible for the disaster.

The Choices

There are two basic political choices which exist regarding nuclear power: the government can withdraw its support for the nuclear power industry, or it can continue to promote nuclear power and encourage its development. We will examine the main arguments which are being presented in this debate.

Withdraw Support for Nuclear Power As the accident at Chernobyl shows, nuclear power plants run the risk of having catastrophic accidents. Society should not have to accept such a risk. The Three Mile Island accident proved that the interaction of human error and failure of equipment can lead to events that no one had ever guessed could happen. One hundred alarms went off in the first few minutes at Three Mile Island, making it impossible for the operators to control the situation. And at Chernobyl a series of errors by the operators of a reactor which was inherently difficult to operate generated forces and effects which up to then had never been experienced. Nuclear technology assumes better human performance and understanding than history shows can be achieved.

Nuclear power increases the danger of the proliferation, or spread, of nuclear weapons to new nations. The knowledge and installations which a nation acquires when it develops nuclear power can be utilized to develop nuclear bombs. While it is true that most nuclear power plants do not use fuel which can readily be used to build bombs, the reprocessing of the spent fuel from the plants can produce fuel for weapons. Reprocessing technology is spreading around the world. For example, in 1975 West Germany sold Brazil reprocessing technology even though Brazil has never signed the Non-proliferation Treaty, which commits nations not to develop nuclear weapons. As more nations gain expertise in nuclear energy, nuclear weapons will be acquired by more of them, thus greatly increasing the chances that the weapons will be used.

The danger of terrorists stealing plutonium to make a bomb or to use as a poison to be spread in the atmosphere over a city or in its drinking water is real. The knowledge of how to make nuclear weapons is widespread, and only about 20 pounds of fissionable material is required to make a crude bomb. If, or probably more realistically when, terrorists do acquire a nuclear capability, threatened nations will probably respond by giving their police and governments increased power. The USA could become more authoritarian because of such a threat, with a consequent restriction of personal freedom and privacy.

Large amounts of radioactive wastes from nuclear power plants are accumulating in the USA because no permanent way to store this material has yet been created. Some of the nuclear waste must be stored for between 100,000 and 200,000 years in such a way that it does not come in contact with humans or with any part of the environment. We show an overwhelming arrogance and unconcern for future generations when we say we can do this; this is made apparent when we remember that the USA is only 200 years old and human civilization about 5,000 years old. Several hundred thousand gallons of nuclear wastes have already leaked out of steel tanks at sites in Hanford, Washington, and near Aiken, South Carolina, where military wastes are stored.

The high cost of nuclear power makes it economically unjustifiable. If one includes the cost of its development and the costs of the attempts to find a safe way to store wastes – both of which have been financed by public funds – nuclear power would not be competitive with other forms of power. And the cost of de-commissioning and possibly hauling away for storage worn out and highly radioactive nuclear power plants, which have a life expect-ancy of 30–40 years, will further add to the costs of nuclear power.

Nuclear power plants create thermal pollution, raising the temperature of the atmosphere and of the water in lakes, bays, and rivers which are often used to cool the reactors. The warmer water is deadly to many kinds of fish and other forms of life in the lakes and rivers. The present light water reactors convert only about 30 percent of their fuel into electricity; the rest is turned into waste heat.

Nuclear power cannot replace imported oil. Only about 10 percent of the world's oil is used to generate electricity; most of it is used to run vehicles, provide heat for homes and industry, and make chemicals. Nuclear power, for the foreseeable future, can be used only to make electricity, and, besides being of relatively limited use, electricity is a very expensive form of energy. The huge public investments which continue to go into nuclear energy prevent public funds from being used to develop alternative sources of energy which would be more useful, safer, and cleaner.

Continue to Support Nuclear Power We accept chemical plants despite accidents associated with them, such as that at Bhopal in India in 1984 which killed more than 2,000 people, and we accept dams despite accidents associated with them, such as that at the Vaiont Dam in Italy in 1963, which also killed about 2,000 people. So why should the accidents at Chernobyl and Three Mile Island make us reject nuclear power? Nuclear power plants in the USA have become much safer because of new procedures and safety devices adopted since the Three Mile Island accident. And a number of highly respected scientists now believe that it is possible to build a nuclear power plant which is inherently safe, one which would be so designed that if anything unusual happened it would automatically cease functioning without any action needed by human beings or machines.

A person gets more exposure to radiation in a year by taking a single round-trip coast-to-coast jet flight, by watching color television, or by working in a building made of granite than she or he would by living next to a nuclear power plant. Humans have evolved over millions of years living on a mildly radioactive planet and have prospered. Few things in life are risk-free, and the risks associated with nuclear power are relatively benign compared with the risks people take every day in their lives.

The accusation that nuclear power will contribute to the proliferation of nuclear weapons is exaggerated. A nation that wants to build a nuclear weapon can get sufficient plutonium from its nuclear research facilities. This is exactly how India got the plutonium for the nuclear device it exploded in 1974. All of the major powers which have acquired nuclear weapons built these weapons before they acquired nuclear power.

It would be very difficult for a terrorist to steal plutonium in the USA. The US military has been shipping plutonium by convoy for many years and very effective means have been devised to protect the shipments from hijacking. Good security measures are also in effect in plants that produce plutonium. Although the knowledge of how to construct nuclear bombs is no longer secret, the actual construction of such a device is very difficult. If the construction of nuclear weapons were easy, more nations would have them than the handful that do at present.

A way to store nuclear wastes permanently has been devised and is actually being used in Europe. The wastes can be solidified, usually in glass, and then stored in geologically stable underground facilities. France has adopted this method, while other European countries have developed other permanent methods. Most of the nuclear wastes in the USA are being created in its military program, and these wastes will continue to build up even if every nuclear power plant should close.

A great danger to the world is caused by the shortage of oil. Without secure sources of energy, such as nuclear power, it is likely that a war will occur as nations fight to keep their sources of oil secure. The development of nuclear power is needed to reduce this dangerous dependency on foreign sources of energy.

Nuclear power is much less polluting than the main alternative energy source – coal – which will be greatly expanded if nuclear power does not continue to be produced. Nuclear power produces no waste gases which cause acid rain, as coal burning does, does not contribute to the build-up of carbon dioxide in the atmosphere, does not produce smog, or any of the other harmful effects commonly associated with coal. Nuclear power is generally much easier on the landscape than is coal; the average nuclear power reactor uses only about 30 tons of fuel a year while the average coal-burning electric plant uses about 3,000 tons of fuel a day. By slowing down the approval of new nuclear plants, the critics of nuclear power are causing nations to burn more coal. This causes many more people to die and more environmental damage from pollution than would have been the case if new nuclear plants had made the increased coal-burning unnecessary.

No energy option should be rejected during this period of transition. Nuclear power is one of the few alternatives we have to produce large amounts of energy during the rest of this century while the search for a sustainable fuel to take the place of oil continues.

CONCLUSIONS

Although the price of oil dropped unexpectedly in the mid-1980s, the long-term prospects for oil remain unchanged. As a non-renewable resource on a planet with a growing population and expanding industrialization, it is a source of energy which will become more scarce and more expensive. Development in the Third World that rests on a petroleum base is as open to disruption as it was in the 1970s when the two oil shocks sent prices shooting upward. Those shocks helped begin the debt crisis which many Third World nations face today as they borrowed to help pay for their higher bills for imported oil. This was a clear warning to the developing nations that their plans to industrialize along the lines followed in the West were based on a faulty assumption, namely, that oil would continue to be available at a low price.

A long-term strategy for the improving of living standards in many poorer nations would seem to call for the development of sources of energy more secure and less costly than oil. The growth-with-equity approach which was presented in chapter 1 advocates the adoption of labor-intensive means of production and alternative technology, both of which would reduce the need for imported oil. Dependency on oil can be reduced also by the adoption of new energy-efficient manufacturing processes. Renewable energy sources such as wood, hydroelectric power, biomass conversion, and solar power offers opportunities for expansion in many Third World nations. The challenge facing the developing nations is to create their needed economic growth without increasing their dependency on oil.

The free market industrialized nations responded fairly well to the increased costs of oil, at least in the short run. The role of prices worked just as the orthodox approach said it would in a capitalist economy. Many industries in the USA gave new attention to ways to make their use of oil more efficient, and succeeded to such a degree that their reduced consumption of oil is one of the factors behind the falling oil prices. New policies by the government also were effective in reducing the demand for oil, such as the required higher fuel efficiency standards for new automobiles and tax benefits for installing new insulation in homes. And especially impressive was the response by millions of individuals in the country who gave up their preference for large, gas-guzzling automobiles and bought small fuel-efficient vehicles. Urgent calls by high governmental officials for Americans to conserve energy had much less effect than did higher prices for gasoline and fuel oil.

But prices work both ways, and a danger exists that lower oil prices in the 1980s will cause many Americans to return to their more energy-profligate ways. One mitigating factor is that many energy conservation actions already taken can not be easily reversed. A home insulated will remain insulated no matter what the attitude of the owner toward energy is now. Another factor which continues to promote conservation in the USA is that, although the price of oil is falling, the price of electricity continues to rise as the huge cost of new nuclear power plants is passed on to consumers.

Disturbing signs exist when one looks at the long-term energy plans of the USA. No plan exists to reduce the dependency of the country on foreign oil. The nuclear energy industry was in the doldrums even before the disaster at Chernobyl. Governmental support for research in solar energy has all but disappeared, and low oil prices are contributing to the lack of interest by private investors in solar research. The recommendation that a tax be placed on imported oil to keep up the incentive to conserve oil is politically unpopular.

In short, the efforts by the leading industrial nation are not impressive in moving forward in this period of energy transition toward an economy based on renewable and non-polluting sources of energy. The needed political leadership in this crucial matter has not yet appeared, which may reflect a lack of awareness by the public that new energy initiatives are needed for the long-term health of the community.

NOTES

1 An interesting discussion of the laws of thermodynamics and what they tell us about energy is contained in Jeremy Rifkin, *Entropy: A New World View* (New York: Viking Press, 1980), pp. 33–43.

2 Daniel Yergin and Martin Hillenbrand (eds), *Global Insecurity: A Strategy for Energy and Economic Renewal* (Boston: Houghton Mifflin, 1982), p. 21.

3 Kenneth M. Dolbeare, *American Public Policy: A Citizen's Guide* (New York: McGraw-Hill, 1982), p. 130.

4 Lester R. Brown, *The Twenty-ninth Day* (New York: W. W. Norton, 1978), pp. 205–6.

5 Yergin and Hillenbrand, *Global Insecurity*, p. 7.

6 Council on Environmental Quality and the Department of State, *Global Future: Time to Act* (Washington, DC: US Government Printing Office, 1981), p. 46.

7 Lester C. Thurow, *The Zero-sum Society: Distribution and Possibilities for Economic Change* (New York: Basic Books, 1980), p. 26.

8 *The New York Times*, late city edn (January 24, 1980, p. 1; July 27, 1983, p. A7).

9 *The New York Times*, late city edn (March 13, 1986), p. D7.

10 Robert C. Weaver, "The Politics of Scarcity," *Proceedings of the Academy of Political Science*, 34 (1981), p. 236.

11 Yergin and Hillenbrand, *Global Insecurity*, p. 11.

12 This analysis is based mainly on that made by Daniel Yergin in Yergin and Hillenbrand, *Global Insecurity*, pp. 11–12.

13 Vaclav Smil, "Ecological Mismanagement in China," *Bulletin of the Atomic Scientists*, 38 (October 1982), p. 19.

14 Ibid., pp. 18–19.

15 Ibid., p. 19.

16 Ibid., p. 20.

17 *The New York Times*, late city edn (November 10, 1981), p. C1.

18 David A. Deese and Joseph S. Nye (eds), *Energy and Security* (Cambridge, Mass.: Ballinger, 1981), p. 112.

19 Ibid., p. 112.

20 As reported in *The New York Times*, national edn (December 6, 1985), p. 34.

21 *The New York Times*, late city edn (May 5, 1986), p. D8. One way Brazil hopes to reduce the amount of oil it imports is by using alcohol to fuel its cars. It is using its huge sugar-cane wastes to produce alcohol and mix this with its gasoline. The country plans eventually to use only alcohol in its automobiles.

22 Wolfgang Sassin, "Energy," *Scientific American*, 243 (September 1980), p. 121; *The New York Times*, late city edn (October 21, 1981), p. 1.

23 Rifkin, *Entropy*, p. 99.

24 UN, *Statistical Yearbook*, 1979/80 (New York: United Nations, 1981), table 189.

25 Most of the US consumption of oil now goes for transportation.

26 The Thunderbird continued to grow in 1975 even though there had been a substantial increase in the price of gasoline. This is explained mainly by the fact that the planning and design of new automobiles takes place several years before the car actually appears on the market for sale.

27 Dennis Pirages, *The New Context for International Relations: Global Ecopolitics* (North Scituate, Mass.: Duxbury Press, 1978), p. 112.

28 *The New York Times*, late city edn (January 25, 1983, p. D1; May 4, 1983, p. D1).

29 Yergin and Hillenbrand, *Global Insecurity*, p. 9.

30 See, for example, the National Research Council, *Energy in Transition 1985–2010* (San Francisco: W. H. Freeman, 1980); Robert Stobaugh and Daniel Yergin (eds), *Energy Future: Report of the Energy Project at the Harvard Business School* (New York: Ballantine Books, 1980); Roger W. Sant, Steven C. Carhard et al., *Eight Great Energy Myths: The Least-cost Energy Strategy – 1978–2000* (Arlington, Va.: Energy Productivity Center of the Mellon Institute, 1981); Solar Energy Research Institute, *A New Prosperity: Building a Sustainable Energy Future* (Andover, Mass.: Brick House Publishing, 1981); National Audubon Society, *Energy Plan* (New York: National Audubon Society, 1981).

31 Council on Environmental Quality and the Department of State, *Global Future*, p. 61.

32 Joel Darmstadter, "Economic Growth and Energy Conservation: Historical and International Lessons," Reprint no. 154 (Washington, DC: Resources for the Future, 1978), p. 18.

33 In 1974 the average fuel efficiency of all American cars was 14 miles per gallon; the law required that this be increased to 27.5 miles per gallon by 1985.

34 Richard J. Barnet, *The Lean Years: Politics in the Age of Scarcity* (New York: Simon and Schuster, 1980), p. 25.

35 Nicholas von Hoffman, " 'Reinventing' America to Save Energy," *New York Times Magazine* (September 23, 1979), p. 62.

36 Council on Environmental Quality, *Global Energy Futures and the Carbon Dioxide Problem* (Washington, DC: Council on Environmental Quality, 1981), p. 1.

37 Rare gases, many of them industrial byproducts, may also be causing the greenhouse effect.

38 Council on Environmental Quality, *Global Energy Futures*, p. 53. Some scientists believe that temperature trends from 1880 to 1980 are consistent with the greenhouse theory. See J. Hansen et al., "Climate Impact of Increasing Atmospheric Carbon Dioxide," *Science*, 213 (August 28, 1981).

39 See, for example, Hansen et al., "Climate Impact," p. 964.

40 Council on Environment Quality, *Global Energy Futures*, p. 6.

41 Ibid., p. 56.

42 Hansen et al., "Climate Impact," p. 966.

43 Council on Environmental Quality, *Global Energy Futures*, pp. 15–18; Hansen et al., "Climate Impact," p. 965.

44 Hansen et al., "Climate Impact," p. 965.

45 Council on Environmental Quality, *Global Energy Futures*, p. 52.

46 Humus, the organic material in top soil, also stores large amounts of carbon.

47 Council on Environmental Quality, *Global Energy Futures*, pp. vii–viii.

48 National Research Council, *Energy in Transition 1985–2010*, p. 129.

49 Ibid., p. 128.

50 Brown, *The Twenty-ninth Day*, p. 119.

51 Council on Environmental Quality and the Department of State, *The Global 2000 Report to the President: Entering the Twenty-first Century*, vol. 1 (New York: Penguin Books, 1982), p. 2.

52 Some analysts argue that the oil companies, which own most of the patents on solar cells, may be delaying the development of solar energy so that they can maximize their profits from fossil fuels. See Ray Reece, *The Sun Betrayed: A Report on the Corporate Seizure of U.S. Solar Energy Development* (Boston: South End Press, 1979), and

Richard Barnet, *The Lean Years: Politics in the Age of Scarcity* (New York: Simon and Schuster, 1980).

53 Barry Commoner, *The Politics of Energy* (New York: Alfred Knopf, 1979).

54 Stobaugh and Yergin, *Energy Future*, p. 10.

55 Ibid., p. 167.

56 Frances Gendlin, "A Talk with Daniel Yergin," *Sierra* (July/August 1981), p. 62.

57 Stobaugh and Yergin, *Energy Future*, p. 198.

58 Quoted in Barnet, *The Lean Years*, p. 100.

59 Paul R. Ehrlich, Anne H. Ehrlich, and John P. Holdren, *Ecoscience: Population, Resources, Environment* (San Francisco: W. H. Freeman, 1977), p. 408–9.

60 Jeremy Bernstein, "Recreating the Power of the Sun," *New York Times Magazine* (January 3, 1982), pp. 14–53.

61 Daniel Yergin, "Troubles of the Atomic Brotherhood," *New York Times Book Review* (July 31, 1983), BR 7.

62 Dorothy Nelkin, "Some Social and Political Dimensions of Nuclear Power: Examples from Three Mile Island," *American Political Science Review*, 75 (March 1981), p. 135.

63 *The New York Times*, late city edn (October 29, 1985), p. D27.

64 *The New York Times*, late city edn (May 30, 1986), p. A9.

65 David Albright, "Chernobyl and the US Nuclear Industry," *Bulletin of the Atomic Scientists*, 42 (November 1986), p. 39.

5

The Environment and Development

We travel together, passengers on a little spaceship,
dependent on its vulnerable resources of air and soil; all
committed for our safety to its security and peace; preserved
from annihilation only by the care, the work, and I will say,
the love we give our fragile craft.

Adlai E. Stevenson (1900–1965)

THE AWAKENING

The relationship between the environment and development has
not been a happy one. Development has often harmed the
environment, and the environmental harm has in turn adversely
affected development. Industrialization brought with it many forms
of pollution, pollution which is undermining the basic biological
systems upon which life rests on this planet. It took millions of
years for these systems to be created.

The current American concern with and awareness of the harm
which is being inflicted on the environment stems from a popular
awakening beginning in the 1960s. Even earlier, some people
warned of the approaching danger. A native American, Chief
Seattle of the Duwamish tribe of the State of Washington, gave the
following warning in the 1800s:

Whatever befalls the earth befalls the sons of the earth. Man
did not weave the web of life; he is merely a strand in it.
Whatever he does to the web, he does to himself.[1]

The first world conference on the environment was held in Stockholm, Sweden, in 1972 under the auspices of the United Nations. At that conference the developed nations, led by the USA, pushed for greater efforts to protect the environment while many less developed nations feared that an effort to create strict anti-pollution laws in their countries would hurt their chances for economic growth. The developing nations maintained that poverty was the main cause of the deterioration of the environment in their countries. What they needed, they said, was more industry instead of less.

Ten years later, the nations of the world again met to discuss the state of the global environment, this time in Nairobi, Kenya. The positions of the rich and poor nations had changed dramatically. The developing nations generally showed enthusiasm for further efforts to protect the environment, since in the ten years between the conferences they had seen that environmental deterioration, such as desertification, soil erosion, deforestation, and the silting of rivers and reservoirs, was harming their efforts to develop and to reduce poverty. On the other hand, many of the rich nations at Nairobi, led by the USA, called for a slowing down of environmental initiatives until they had recovered from their economic recessions.

Even though the positions of the developed and developing nations had become somewhat reversed during the ten years between the two environmental conferences, there is no doubt that an awareness of the threat to the environment caused by human activities has now become world-wide. Only 11 nations had any kind of governmental environmental agency at the time of the first conference, whereas over 100 nations, 70 of them in the Third World, had such agencies at the time of the second. These agencies are doing much to educate their own governments and people about environmental dangers.

In this chapter we will examine some of the effects development has had on the air, water, and land of our planet. We will then focus on some of the dangers that have been created in the workplace and in the home. After looking briefly at the use of natural resources in the world, we will learn why the extinction of species is accelerating. The chapter will end with an explanation of what makes environmental politics so controversial.

THE AIR

Pollution

Industrialization everywhere has brought dirtier air. From factories and transportation systems, with their tell-tale smoke stacks and exhaust pipes, toxic fumes are emitted into the air. In a few spectacular instances in various countries in the twentieth century large numbers of people have become ill or died because of the toxic gases in the air they breathed: 6,000 became ill and 60 died in the Meuse Valley in Belgium in 1930; 6,000 became ill and 20 died in Donora, Pennsylvannia, in 1948; and in London tens of thousands became ill and 4,000 died in 1952.[2] (It was this last-mentioned instance which led the United Kingdom to pass various laws to clean up the air which have proved to be quite successful. In the late 1970s, 80 per cent more sunshine reached London than had in 1952.[3]) In 1984 an accidental release of toxic gas from an American-owned chemical plant in Bhopal, India, killed about 2,000 people and injured 200,000.

A number of industrialized countries, including the USA, have made significant progress in reducing air pollution in their large urban areas, but much remains to be done. In the early 1980s the air in most large US cities was still considered poor enough to be called unhealthy during some days of the year. The American city with the worst air, Los Angeles, had about 240 unhealthy days in 1981, with more than 100 being considered very unhealthy.[4] Third World countries that were starting to industrialize and modernize were facing air pollution problems not unlike those of the West. Cities such as Calcutta, Caracas, Ankara, Seoul, and Mexico City were experiencing serious smog problems, caused partly by their increasing numbers of automobiles. And one Third World city, Cubatao, in southern Brazil, earned the reputation as having possibly the worst air in the world. This city, with its numerous Brazilian and foreign factories, had air so contaminated that no birds, butterflies, or other insects existed in the city. Forty out of every 1,000 babies there were born dead and another 40 died within a week. Most of the infants who died were deformed.[5]

Airborne Lead

The story of airborne lead illustrates well the connection between industrialization and air pollution. Scientists are able to estimate the amount of lead there was in the world's air in the past by taking core samples of the ice in the Greenland ice cap. The ice, which represents past rainfall, shows that from 800 BC to the beginning of the Industrial Revolution around 1750, the amount of lead in the air was low. There was a major increase after 1750 and a huge increase after World War II when the use of leaded gasoline rose sharply. In 1965 the lead concentration in the Greenland ice was 400 times higher than the level in 800 BC. Other studies show that the bones of today's Americans contain 500 times more lead than those of prehistoric humans.[6]

Children are the ones who are most susceptible to harm from breathing lead. They inhale two to three times as much lead in the air per unit of body weight as do adults because their metabolic rates are higher and they have greater physical activity than adults. There is no known safe level of lead in the human body. High levels of lead poisoning can lead to death, but even low levels can cause learning difficulties and behavioral problems. In the early 1980s about 5 percent of preschool children in America had high levels of lead in their blood, and black children were more likely to have high levels of lead than were white children.[7]

A significant improvement in reducing the amount of lead in the blood of Americans came in the late 1970s, when the average amount of lead fell by about 40 percent in just four years.[8] Because of tighter federal government air pollution requirements, new cars were required to use non-leaded gasoline, and many experts believe that the reduced use of leaded gasoline is probably the cause of the lower lead levels in blood. In 1985 the US Environmental Protection Agency instructed oil companies to reduce the amount of lead in gasoline by 90 per cent by the end of the year, and was considering ordering a total ban on leaded gasoline in 1988.

Acid Rain

When fossil fuels are burned, sulfur dioxide and oxides of nitrogen are released into the air. As these gases react with other chemicals and with sunlight and moisture in the atmosphere, the sulfur dioxide becomes sulfuric acid (the same substance that is used in car batteries) and the oxides of nitrogen become nitric acid. These acids then return to earth in rain, snow, hail, or fog. When they do, they can kill fish in lakes and streams, dissolve limestone statues and gravestones, corrode metal, and possibly kill certain trees and reduce the growth of some crops. The effects of acid rain on human health are not yet known. Some scientists fear that it could help dissolve toxic metals in water pipes and in the soil, releasing these metals into human water supplies.

In the USA, acid rain comes mainly from sulfur dioxide produced by coal-burning electricity-generating power plants in the Midwest and from the nitrogen oxides from auto and truck exhausts. It has caused lakes in the northeastern part of the country to become so acidic that fish and some other forms of life are unable to live in them. Other areas of the country, such as large parts of the South, Northwest, Rocky Mountains, and the northern Midwest, are especially sensitive to acid rain since the land and lakes in these areas contain a low amount of lime. Lime tends to neutralize the falling acid. An international dispute has been created between Canada and the USA since a large amount of the acid rain falling on huge sections of Canada comes from industrial emissions in the USA.

Europe is facing a similar problem. Many lakes in Norway and Sweden are now so acidic that fish cannot live in them and about one-third of the forests in Germany are sick and dying. Much of the acid rain falling in northern and central Europe comes from industry in Britain, Germany, and France.

Acid rain was first observed in industrial England in the late 1800s, but nothing was done about it. The response to the increasing air pollution in the USA and Europe in the 1950s was to build tall smokestacks on factories so that emissions of toxic gases would be dispersed by the air currents into the atmosphere. These tall smokestacks led to a noticeable improvement in the air around many factories, smelters, power plants, and refineries, but the dispersal of noxious gases in the atmosphere gave more time for these gases to form into acid rain. We are now realizing that the tall smokestacks violated a fundamental law of ecology, one that biologist Barry Commoner has labeled the "everything must go somewhere" law.[9] Matter is indestructible, and there are no "wastes" in nature. What is excreted by one organism as waste is absorbed by another as food. When the food is toxic, the organism dies. Thus is explained the beautiful clear water in lakes with a high acid content: many forms of plankton, insects, and plants have ceased to exist there.

A 1983 study by the National Academy of Sciences concluded that acid rain could be curbed if sulfur dioxide emissions were reduced from coal-burning power plants and factories.[10] In 1984 nine European countries and Canada agreed to reduce sulfur dioxide emissions by at least 30 percent in the next decade. The USA, Britain, East Germany, Poland, and Czechoslovakia refused to join in this agreement. The position of the Reagan administration at that time was that further scientific study was needed before costly action was taken. In 1986 the USA promised Canada that it would undertake a $5 billion research effort over the next five years to develop cleaner coal-burning technology.

Ozone Depletion

The ozone layer in the atmosphere protects the earth from harmful ultraviolet rays from the sun. Most scientists believe that life on earth did not evolve until the ozone layer was established. That layer is now being reduced by substances produced by humans, mainly in the developed nations. Chloro-fluorocarbons, used as a propellant in aerosol spray cans, as a fluid in refrigerators and air conditioners, and for other industrial purposes, can destroy ozone, as can exhaust gases from supersonic transport planes. Ozone may also be destroyed by gases which are released when nitrogen fertilizer is extensively used and when nuclear bombs are exploded. The USA and a few other developed nations have now banned the use of chloro-fluorocarbons in aerosol cans, but other uses of the substance world-wide were increasing by 7 percent a year in the early 1980s, a percentage that would lead to a doubling in use if continued for ten years.[11]

Scientists are agreed that any major depletion of the ozone layer would cause serious harm to humans, other mammals, plants, birds, insects, and some sea life. Skin cancer would increase, as would damage to the eyes of living creatures, including humans. As will be mentioned in the chapter on technology, one of the most harmful effects of a nuclear war would be the damage it would do to the ozone layer, which would affect life far beyond the combat area.

By analyzing past data, British scientists in the mid-1980s discovered that, during two months of the year, a hole was occurring in the ozone layer over the South Pole. The hole appears to be growing each year, and in 1985 it was about the size equivalent to the area of the USA. Some scientists are concerned that if this phenomenon proves to be a permanent feature instead of a temporary one, and to be caused by human actions instead of by natural forces, it could indicate that the danger to the ozone layer is much greater than has been assumed up to now.

Carbon Dioxide

The release of carbon dioxide into the atmosphere from the burning of fossil fuels may be causing a warming of the earth's climate. This warming, called the greenhouse effect, has been discussed in chapter 4 above. The current trend in the USA and some other industrial countries to return to the use of coal because of the high price and unreliable supplies of oil will extend their reliance on fossil fuels for energy, thus invariably leading to an increased release of carbon dioxide. No affordable technology exists at present to prevent the release of carbon dioxide when fossil fuels are burned.

THE WATER

Development, to date, has tended to turn clean water into dirty water as often as it has turned fresh air into dirty air. In the USA the deterioration of the nation's rivers was dramatized in the late 1960s when the Cuyahoga River, which flows through Cleveland, caught fire because it was so polluted. That event helped prod the US Congress into passing a law in the early 1970s which set a ten-year goal to return the nation's waterways to a state where they would be "fishable, and swimmable." Ten years after the Clean Water Act of 1972, many US rivers, streams, and lakes were cleaner than they were when the Act was passed, but many remained too polluted to allow safe fishing or swimming. This was illustrated by the recommendation that the State of New York's Department of Health made to the state's residents in 1983. The Department recommended that they should eat no more than one meal a month of fresh-water fish caught in the state and that pregnant women, women of child-bearing age, nursing mothers, and children under 15 should eat no fish at all from the state![12]

Less progress was made in cleaning up the water than the air, since the problem turned out to be much more complicated and costly than had been anticipated. Significant progress was made in reducing water pollution from sewage produced by cities and factories as billions of dollars were spent on building new sewage treatment plants, but little progress was made in reducing the pollution from urban and agricultural runoffs. Especially during storms, huge amounts of polluted water drain from cities directly into rivers and lakes, untreated by local sewage treatment plants, and huge amounts of water drain from farms laden with pesticides, herbicides, and excess fertilizers.

Other developed countries have also experienced serious water pollution problems. As Lester Brown has nicely put it, if Johann Strauss were to write his famous waltz today he would have to call it the "Brown Danube." The Danube, which flows through central Europe, was so badly polluted in the late 1970s that it was illegal to swim in it, and the Rhine, even after billions had been spent to clean it up, was still considered the world's dirtiest river.[13] The Soviet Union, whose government-controlled press in the past did not make public reports about pollution in that country, is now considered by certain environmentalists to have some of the most severe environmental problems of any developed country, including serious water pollution problems.[14] One exception to the rather gloomy picture in Europe is the Thames, which flows through London. Once known as being a very filthy river, it has been cleaned up to such an extent that fish have now returned to it.

What is causing the polluted water in the developed nations? Industry must take a large part of the blame since traditionally industrial wastes have been dumped into nearby water as often as into the air overhead. Many industries are no longer dumping wastes into nearby rivers, but some dumping still goes on. The source of much of the most serious water pollution today in the developed countries is chemicals. The chemical industry has had a huge growth in the industrial world since World War II. Chemicals are now finding their way into waterways, many of which are being used for drinking water. A study by the US Environmental Protection Agency (EPA) in the mid-1970s found that water supplies of 80 American cities contained chemicals that may cause cancer.[15]

In addition to the problem of the unsafe disposal of wastes by the chemical industry, which will be discussed in the next section of this chapter, many of the 50,000 different chemicals which the US chemical industry is producing are not now being disposed of by consumers in a manner that avoids contaminating water supplies. An especially dangerous fact is the discovery that about one-half of the underground water upon which about 100 million Americans depend for all or some of their drinking water is threatened with chemical contamination or is already contaminated.[16] These underground aquifers, some of which took millions of years to form, were once thought to be safe from pollution, but it is now recognized they are threatened. Toxic wastes have been found in the groundwater of at least 34 states.[17] Once these waters are contaminated it is extremely difficult, and many times impossible, to remove the contamination. The groundwater aquifers are replenished slowly from the land above. When that land is contaminated by suburban cesspools, industrial wastes, and chemicals used on farms, the groundwater becomes polluted. The experience of communities on New York State's Long Island was that, after the land above the aquifer was urbanized, it took about 20 years for the aquifers, from which many of these communities got their drinking water, to become contaminated.[18]

The US Government's *Global 2000 Report* projects that the demands for fresh water in the world will increase by 200–300 percent from 1975 to the year 2000. Population growth alone will lead to a doubling in the demands for fresh water in half the countries of the world.[19] The largest user of water is agriculture, which takes 70–80 percent of that used by humans. Agribusiness uses a huge amount of water for irrigation, and its demands are expected to grow as industrial farming techniques continue to spread in the USA and the Green Revolution spreads around the world. Except for regional and temporary shortages, the USA has never had a shortage of fresh water; indeed, Americans are as profligate in their use of water as they used to be of oil before the oil shocks. The situation may change as heavy demands on fresh water by agriculture occur. The continued development of states like Nevada and Arizona has led to such extensive pumping of groundwater that the land is sinking (4 feet in Las Vegas in only 20 years) and huge cracks are opening up in the land (some near Phoenix). In the Third World, widespread deforestation will make water supplies more erratic and growing populations will undoubtedly lead to new conflicts over the availability of water, such as have taken place in the past between India and Pakistan, Israel and Syria, and Mexico and the USA.

THE LAND

Whenever development has occurred, its effect on the land has been profound. The economic growth that comes with development increases the amount of goods and services available for human consumption. More natural resources from the land are required for the production of these goods, of course, and their extraction disturbs the land greatly. But even more widespread are the changes to the land which come with the disposal of the goods after they are no longer of use, and of the wastes which were created in the manufacture of the goods. Many of these wastes are artificial substances which never existed before in nature; thus nature has few, if any, ways of breaking them down into harmless substances. Development also affects the vegetation on the land, in some ways reducing it and in some ways helping to preserve it. In this section we will focus on two of the many changes to the land that come with development: the disposal of wastes and deforestation. These two changes are affecting many human beings in such direct ways today that it is well that we look at them closely.

Solid Wastes

It seems to be a common occurrence in a number of developed countries that, as more goods and services become available, more are desired and less value is placed on those already in hand. After the end of World War II, an unprecedented period of economic growth in the industrialized world took place, leading to a huge increase in the consumption of material goods.

As consumption rose so did wastes. "Throw-away" products that were used briefly and then discarded became common in the USA. Commonly produced also was the item that wore out quickly, a fact that disturbed few Americans since they found enjoyment in buying new, "better" products. Many such products were relatively cheap in the 1950s, 1960s, and early 1970s since energy and other raw materials were inexpensive. Around 1970 the average American was discarding 200 pounds of paper, 250 metal cans, 130 bottles and jars, and, on a national basis, 7 million cars and 100 million tires per year.[20]

Besides bringing ugliness to the land, the wastes soon wrought other changes, changes to the health of people who inadvertently came into contact with them. Toxic wastes became the environmental problem of the 1980s in the USA as thousands found that their health was, or was possibly, being affected by chemical wastes. These wastes came after World War II from the manufacture of many new products from chemicals – everything from new fabrics, deodorants, toothpastes, and plastic containers to new drugs, pesticides, and fertilizers.

Toxic Wastes

The first warning of the danger of toxic wastes came from Japan. In the 1950s and 1960s hundreds of people were paralyzed, crippled, or killed from eating fish contaminated by mercury which had been discharged into Minamata Bay by a chemical plant. In the late 1970s the warning came to the USA. Many people in a residential district of Niagara Falls, New York, were exposed to a dangerous mixture of chemicals which was seeping into their swimming pools and basements. Most of these people did not know, when they bought their homes, that the Hooker Chemical Company had dumped over 20,000 tons of chemical wastes in the 1940s and 1950s into a nearby abandoned canal, ironically known as Love Canal. News of the Love Canal disaster spread through the country as the story of the contamination slowly came out in spite of the denials of the chemical company and the apathy of the local government.[21] Eventually hundreds of people were evacuated from the area. The state and federal governments bought over 600 of the contaminated homes.

Love Canal is undoubtedly the tip of the iceberg. Between 250 and 290 million metric tons of hazardous wastes were being generated in the USA yearly in the early 1980s.[22] In 1980 the EPA estimated that only about 10 percent of the hazardous wastes produced in the country were being disposed of in environmentally safe ways.[23] Seventy percent of these wastes come from the chemical industry. Much of them are being stored in unlined lagoons, injected into deep wells, spread on the ground, dumped into sewers, placed in solid waste dumps, and incinerated in unsafe ways. In Missouri, residents found to their distress that waste oil mixed with the highly toxic chemical dioxin had been sprayed on many of the state's roads and horse arenas in the 1970s to keep down dust. The federal government bought the Missouri town of Times Beach since so much of it was contaminated.[24] Since there are over 15,000 hazardous waste dumps and landfills in the country, the efforts to clean up the most dangerous ones represent a huge undertaking by both government and industry.

Governmental and Industrial Responses to the Waste Problem

In 1980 the US government created a $1.6 billion fund to finance the cleaning up of the worst toxic waste sites. The law that set up this fund allowed the government to recover the cost of the clean-up from the companies that dumped wastes at the sites. In 1986 $9 billion more for the clean-up was approved by the US government, to come mainly from a broadly based tax on industry and a tax on crude oil. The Congressional Office of Technology Assessment has estimated that it will require about 50 years and $100 billion to clean up toxic waste dumps in the country.[25]

There are other ways government can help control the waste problem. Barbara Ward, the late British economist, mentions four ways a government can encourage the reduction of wastes and promote the reuse of wastes: (1) it can make manufacturers pay a tax which could cover the cost of handling the eventual disposal of their products; (2) it could stimulate the market for recycled products by purchasing recycled products for some of its own needs; (3) it could give grants and other incentives to cities and industries to help them install equipment which recycles wastes; and (4) it could prohibit the production of non-returnable containers in some instances.[26] The last-mentioned device has been used by nine states in the USA. They have effectively banned nonreturnable (throw-away) beer and soft drink containers, and are getting about 90 percent of the refillable containers recycled.[27]

Inefficient and wasteful technologies and processes to produce goods are still common in the USA and other developed nations, since many of these were adopted when energy was cheap, water plentiful, many raw materials inexpensive, and the disposal of wastes easy. Some industries now realize that they can increase their profits by making their procedures more efficient and producing less wastes. One such company is 3M, which, according to one study, has reduced its pollution as well as increased its profits, "not by installing pollution control plants but by re-formulating products, redesigning equipment, modifying processes . . . [and] recovering materials for reuse."[28]

Deforestation

It is estimated that, if present trends continue, 10–15 percent of the tropical forests – much of the last remaining large forests in the world – will be gone by the year 2000.[29] In most poor countries that are undergoing a large growth of population and still have sizeable forests, deforestation is progressing rapidly. Only South Korea and China in the Third World have increased their forests recently, and in China the planting of new forests in some parts of the country has taken place at the same time serious deforestation has occurred in other parts. Only in the developed nations of North America and Europe, including the Soviet Union, are the forests fairly stable.

Deforestation is a serious problem because it leads to erosion of the land, can cause the soil to harden, and makes the supply of fresh water erratic. Recent scientific studies support the hypothesis that deforestation can lead to significant changes in the climate. These changes usually mean less rainfall.[30] Sometimes deforestation leads to too much water in the wrong places. Serious floods are occurring now in India in areas where there were never floods before; it is believed that the cutting of forests in the Himalaya Mountains, the watershed for many rivers in India, is causing the flooding. Rioting has even been reported among some of the tribal peoples of India who are protesting the cutting of their forests by commercial firms.

Most of the destruction of the tropical rain forests, however, is carried out not by commercial logging firms, although they do a significant amount of cutting, but by small-scale farmers.[31] Other forest destruction has been conducted for colonization purposes and to create pastures for cattle raising. In the early 1970s the Brazilian government began a large colonization project in the Amazon basin, moving people in from the poverty-ridden north-eastern section of the country. It was hoped that the resettlements would help reduce the poverty in the northeast and provide food for an expanding population. Unfortunately, both hopes faded as colony after colony failed. The main reason for the failure was that tropical forest land is actually not very fertile, in spite of the huge trees growing on it. In many places the top soil is thin and of poor quality; the trees get their needed nutrients directly from decaying leaves and wood on the forest floor and not from the soil. This fact explains why many of the settlers had experiences similar to that of the following Brazilian peasant who described what happened to his new farm in the Amazon:

The bananas were two feet long the first year. They were one foot long the second year. And six inches long the third year. The fourth year? No bananas.[32]

Some scientists now believe that the mysterious decline of several great civilizations in the past, such as the Khmer civilization in Southeast Asia and the Mayan civilization in Central America, was caused by over-intensive agriculture on basically fragile land. And recent research supports the theory that the total deforestation of Easter Island, where a former civilization carved over 600 huge stone heads, was the direct cause of the collapse of that civilization since it led to the loss of fertile soils and fuel.[33]

The cutting of the trees in a tropical forest puts a severe strain on the soil since the trees protect the soil from the violent rains which are common in the tropics. And once the soil is washed away, it is not easily recreated. Some studies now estimate that from 100 to 1,000 years is needed for a mature tropical forest to return after human disturbances have taken place.[34]

If only small plots of the forest are cleared, regeneration of the forest is possible. Some peoples have practiced what is known as shifting cultivation in the tropical forests. They clear a piece of land and farm it for a year or two before moving on to a new piece of land. As long as this remains small-scale, the damage to the forest is limited, but any large-scale use of this type of agriculture can lead to irreversible damage to the forest.

Some tropical soils contain a layer known as laterite, which is rich in iron. When these soils are kept moist under a forest they remain soft, but if allowed to dry out, which happens when the forest cover is removed, they become irreversibly hard – so hard that the soil is sometimes used for making bricks.

There is a danger that the destruction of forests will contribute to the greenhouse effect. Trees that are burned after they are cut, which is common when the forest land is cleared for settlements or for farming, release carbon dioxide into the atmosphere. The great tropical rain forests contain a huge reservoir of carbon and have been described by some as the "lungs" of the earth, absorbing carbon dioxide and releasing oxygen.

In Central America and in Brazil, large areas of forests are being cut down to make pastures for the raising of cattle. The cattle are being raised mainly to supply the fast food hamburger market in the USA. The growing of cattle on large ranches for export does not, of course, do anything to solve the food problems in the exporting countries, or to provide land to the landless.

It is mainly the landless and poor around the world today who are assaulting the remaining forests for agricultural land and fuel. As poverty is the root cause of the hunger problem which was discussed in chapter 3, and one of the root causes of the population explosion discussed in chapter 2, so also is it at the root of the deforestation problem. Development can reduce poverty, and when it does this for the multitude – as the growth-with-equity theory, which was presented in chapter 1, advocates – it can reduce the threat to the world's forests. Development can also lead to the destruction of the forests as they are cleared for cattle farms, for lumber, for commercial ventures, and for human settlements. As with the population problem, development in its early stages seems to worsen the situation; but development which benefits the many and not just the few can eventually help relieve it.

THE WORKPLACE AND THE HOME

Cancer

It is estimated that one out of four Americans alive at present will contract cancer and many of these will die from it.[35] Cancer now kills more children than any other disease, although accidents are still the number one cause of death of children. It is commonly believed by the general public that exposure of workers to cancer-causing substances – carcinogens – in the workplace, and the exposure of the general population to pollution in the air and water and to carcinogens in some of the food they eat, are the main causes of this dreaded disease. There is no question that many workers have been exposed to dangerous substances, which is probably the cause of the high levels of cancer among them – such as the millions of people who worked with asbestos. But scientists do not now believe that contamination at the workplace is the main cause of cancer; nor do they believe that air and water pollution or food additives are causing most of the cancer cases. The consensus among leading cancer experts at present is that smoking and diet, mainly a high-animal-fat and low-fiber diet, are the main causes.[36] Some experts, however, fear that, while chemicals cannot be blamed for most cancer today, there is a possibility that chemical-related cancers may increase greatly in the future because of the large increase in the production of carcinogenic chemicals since the 1960s. Cancer can occur 15–40 years after the initial exposure to a carcinogen, so chemicals may yet prove to be a major culprit.

Pesticides

The story of pesticide use illustrates well the dangers that new substances, which have become so important to modern agriculture, have brought to people at their workplace as well as in their homes at mealtime. Rachel Carson is credited with making a whole nation aware of the dangers of persistent pesticides such as DDT. Her book, *Silent Spring*, which appeared in 1962, shows how toxic substances are concentrated as they go up the food chain, as big animals eat little animals. Since most of the toxic substances are not excreted by the fish or animal absorbing them, they accumulate and are passed on to the higher animal in a concentrated form. Carson's warning led to a sharp reduction in the use of long-lived pesticides in many developed countries; but if she were alive today (she died of cancer in 1964), she would probably be disturbed to learn that short-lived, but highly toxic, pesticides are now increasing in use in the USA. The use of herbicides has especially increased dramatically as farmers, railroad companies, telephone companies, and others find it cheaper and easier to use these chemicals to get rid of unwanted vegetation than by using labor or machines. These new highly toxic pesticides place a special risk on the workers who manufacture them and on the farmers who work with them in the fields.

Pesticide use is increasing in the less developed nations – not just the use of short-lived pesticides, but the use of persistent pesticides such as DDT as well. Of the pesticides produced in the USA for export, 25 percent are substances that are banned, highly restricted, or unregistered in the USA.[37] US law explicitly permits the sale of these substances to foreign nations, and US companies, as well as many in Europe, have increasingly turned to the overseas market to sell their products as more restrictions on the use of pesticides occur in the developed nations.

The World Health Organization estimates that half a million people are poisoned yearly by exported pesticides, and that most of these people live in Third World countries.[38] Many farm laborers in developing countries who are using the pesticides are illiterate and cannot understand the warnings on the pesticide containers. Many other workers, such as in the cotton fields in Central America, end up having themselves, their water supplies, and their homes, which are often near the fields, sprayed with pesticides from the air, some as many as 40 times during a growing season. In the late 1970s Guatemalan women living in cotton-growing areas had the highest concentration of DDT in their breast milk ever found in the Western world.[39] Tropical fruits being grown for export are sprayed heavily to keep them free of blemishes. A vicious circle is created in which the heavy use of pesticides leads to the killing off of natural predators and the evolving of pests which are resistant to the pesticide, which in turn leads the farmer to turn to new and more toxic pesticides.

Many of the agricultural products on which banned pesticides are being used are imported into the USA. The US Food and Drug Administration (FDA) estimates that at least 10 percent of the food coming into the country has illegally high residues of pesticides on it.[40] And it is believed that the real percentage of imported contaminated food is much higher than the FDA estimates because the Administration does not test for many contaminants. The FDA finds mysterious, unknown chemicals on the foods at times, which is not surprising, since chemical companies are permitted to export unregistered pesticides, pesticides that have never been tested by the government. Illegally high residues of pesticides have been found on imported meat, coffee, beans, peppers, and cabbages. Many of these products are sold in American supermarkets before the FDA tests on them are completed.

The US Department of Agriculture has estimated that 32 percent of US crops were lost to pests in 1945 whereas in 1984, despite a large increase in the use of pesticides, the loss due to pests had risen to 37 percent.[41] This situation may explain why a number of agricultural experts are now advocating a more balanced program for controlling pests. A selective use of pesticides would go along with the use of biological controls, such as natural predators, and other nonchemical means to control pests.

Pesticides have played an important role in the successes of the Green Revolution; it is doubtful that food production would have stayed ahead of population growth in the world without them. What seems to be called for now is a highly selective use of pesticides, not their banishment.

Artificial Substances

Development has led to the introduction of many artificial substances that have never been adequately tested to verify their safety. The National Research Council of the National Academy of Sciences concluded, after a three-year study in the mid-1980s, that tens of thousands of important chemicals had never been fully tested for potential health hazards. The Council found that this included about 90 percent of the chemicals used in commerce, 60 percent of the ingredients in drugs, 65 percent of pesticide ingredients, 85 percent of cosmetic ingredients, and 80 percent of food additives.[42] The general conclusion of the Counc̲ have a substantial ignorance about many products contact with in our lives today.

Not everything causes cancer, of course, but deve brought forth so many new products in such a short can't be sure which ones do and which don't. Barry Commoner shows that new products often bring large profits to the first industry which introduces them, so there is a strong incentive for industries to be innovative. The new products, especially in the USA since World War II, are often made of synthetic materials which pollute the environment, but the pollution usually does not become evident until years after the introduction. Commoner states that, "by the time the effects are known, the damage is done and the inertia of the heavy investment in a new productive technology makes a retreat extraordinarily difficult."[43]

THE USE OF NATURAL RESOURCES

Since the world's population is growing exponentially, as we learned in chapter 2, it is probably not surprising that the production and consumption of nonfuel minerals are also growing exponentially. But, unlike petroleum, the supplies of minerals are not becoming exhausted. In fact, the known reserves of all major minerals actually increased between 1950 and 1980 as more deposits of ores were discovered.[44] Another great difference between nonfuel natural resources and energy supplies is that the actual cost of producing most minerals has decreased over the past century.[45] This reduced cost has occurred, even as lower-grade ores are being mined, because of advances in technology – such as better exploration techniques, bigger mechanical shovels to dig with, bigger trucks to haul the ore away, and bigger ships to transport it to processing plants. Whether new technology will continue to keep the cost of minerals low in the future is a subject that is debated by scientists and economists. As ores which contain a lower concentration of the desired minerals are mined and less accessible deposits are turned to, processing costs will rise. Also, mineral extraction is highly energy-intensive, and rising energy costs will directly affect the price of minerals. Some analysts have observed that mineral prices in the past did not reflect the true environmental ɔsts of extracting and processing the minerals, but with new pollution laws in most industrial countries, the mining industry will have to assume more of these costs.

One trend that is apparent is that the industrialized nations, with the exception of the USSR, are becoming more dependent on foreign countries for their minerals. The USA is a mineral-rich country; in the 1950s it was nearly self-sufficient in the most important industrial minerals. Now, it is self-sufficient in only seven of the 36 minerals essential to an industrial society, whereas the Soviet Union is estimated to be self-sufficient in 26.[46] Western Europe and Japan are even more dependent on imported minerals than is the USA. This increasing dependency on ores from foreign countries, many of which are essential for the advanced technologies common in the USA, have strongly influenced US foreign policy toward the Third World, where many of the minerals are found.

There are four main steps a country can take to counteract shortages of a needed material if it cannot locate new rich deposits of the ore: (1) it can recycle waste products containing the desired material; (2) it can substitute more abundant or renewable resources for the scarce material; (3) it can turn to ore deposits which have a lower concentration of the needed mineral; or (4) it can reduce its needs for the material. All of these options have some negative features.

Recycling

It is generally agreed that more recycling of waste material needs to be done in the USA. Relatively little is done at present. As has been mentioned, a "throw-away" economy developed after World War II, and it still exists.

Government policies discriminate against recycled material in the USA, sometimes inadvertently. The Interstate Commerce Commission allows freight rates for scrap metal that are three times higher than rates for iron ore. Various tax benefits, such as depletion allowances, are given to some mining industries. The reluctance to recycle scrap metal contributes to the energy crisis discussed in the chapter on energy since steel made from scrap metal requires one-third as much energy as that made from virgin ore (the comparable figure for aluminium is one-twentieth).[47]

Sweden is a country which encourages recycling. It promotes the recycling of old automobiles by imposing a disposal tax on each new car sold which is refunded to the owner when the car is turned in to a scrap yard.

While recycling is desirable, it is only a partial solution to resource shortages and to pollution by the minerals industry. Recycling also creates pollution and uses energy. It is currently only about 30 percent efficient for most used metals.[48] The move by the American soft drink and beer industry to use throwaway aluminium cans that can be recycled is obviously not the final solution to the litter problem. A significant number of the aluminium cans are never collected for recycling, and the manufacture of aluminium uses a lot of energy. Probably a better solution was the move by some states, as mentioned above, to require returnable soft drink and beer containers to be used in their states instead of throwaways. Oregon's experience with its container law has been that highway litter was significantly reduced, recycling was stimulated, the price of beverages remained about the same, and new jobs were created.[49]

Substitution

When a material becomes scarce, it is sometimes possible to substitute another material for it which is more abundant or to use a renewable resource in place of the scarce item. For example, the more abundant aluminium can be used in place of the more scarce copper for most electrical uses. Difficulties arise at times when the substituted material in turn becomes scarce. Plastic utensils and containers replaced glass products in most American kitchens because of certain advantages plastic has over glass, such as being less breakable and light in weight. But plastics are made from petrochemicals, which are now becoming scarcer. Also, the plastics industry produces more dangerous pollutants than does the glass industry. Another limitation to substitution is that some materials have unique qualities which no other materials have. Tungsten's high melting point, for example, is unmatched by any other metal. And substitutions can produce disruptions in the society, causing some industries to close and new ones to open. The last-mentioned point can mean, of course, new opportunities for some people and fewer for others. New ways of doing things can also be substituted for old ways, sometimes resulting in a reduced use of resources. The trend in some businesses to use communications in place of transportation (business meetings with participants on video screens instead of their physically being present) might be such a development.

Mining of Low-grade Ores

Many of the deposits with the highest concentration of the desired minerals have now been mined, but there are large, less rich deposits of many desired minerals scattered around the world. These can be, and in many places are, mined. There are significant costs incurred when such mining takes place. The cost increases, since more ore must be processed, mines must be bigger, and more energy and water must be used. Because more ore must be processed, more wastes are produced. Large strip mines have a devastating effect on the land, of course, and even the best attempts to restore the land, which are costly, are very imperfect.

Reducing Needs

Many consumer goods in the USA become obsolete in a few years as styles change, such as with automobiles and clothes. This planned obsolescence leads to a high use of resources. Many products also wear out quickly and must be replaced with new ones. More durable products could be designed by American industry, but they would often be more expensive. It is probably for this reason that American industry generally doesn't make such products. Higher prices would mean fewer sales, a slower turnover of business inventories, and thus lower profits. They could also mean fewer jobs.

Perhaps a good way to end this section is to explain the concept of overdevelopment. According to the Australian biologist Charles Birch, "overdevelopment of any country starts when the citizens of that country consume resources and pollute the environment at a rate which is greater than the world could stand indefinitely if all the peoples of the world consumed resources at that rate."[50] By using the perspective of this concept, it can be seen that the USA could be considered the most overdeveloped country in the world, followed closely by many other industrial countries. Americans, who constitute about 5 percent of the world's population, consume about 30 percent of the world's production of materials, and do so, as this chapter has shown, with devastating effects on the environment. This is changing as new environmental laws are enacted and gradually enforced in the developed world, but it has not altered to such an extent to make the concept of over-development outdated.

THE EXTINCTION OF SPECIES

There are approximately 5–10 million species of living things on earth. Throughout the earth's history, new species have evolved and others have become extinct, with the general trend being that more new species are created than die out. It is now believed that because of human actions this trend has been reversed, with extinctions outnumbering the creation of new species. And the trend appears to be increasing. Ecologist Norman Myers estimates that one species now becomes extinct every day, and that by the end of the 1980s the rate of extinction could increase to one per hour. By the year 2000, Myers estimates that one million species could be extinct.[51]

Whereas hunting used to be the main way humans caused extinction, it is now generally believed that the destruction of natural habitats is the principal cause of extinctions. As the human population grows, humans exploit new areas of the world for economic gain and often destroy life forms as they do so.

A dramatic example of how habitats are destroyed can be seen by looking at a development scheme in the Amazon valley. The tropical rain forests, of which the Amazon is the largest, harbor up to three-quarters of the species on earth. The year-round warm temperature, heavy rainfall, and prevalent sunlight produce excellent conditions for the evolution of species. Such species can be destroyed when the land is cleared to make way for farms and commercial enterprises, such as the large land development scheme known as "Jari."

In the late 1960s, the American shipping executive and financier Daniel Ludwig, one of the richest persons in the USA, purchased a parcel of land in the Brazilian Amazon approximately the size of the state of Connecticut. Ludwig invested about $1 billion to construct a paper-pulp factory there. (The factory and a wood-burning power plant were constructed in Japan and towed to the Amazon on huge barges.) Large parts of the forest on Ludwig's estate were cut down and burned to make way for the planting of two or three species of fast-growing trees he brought into the area. As Ludwig said, "I always wanted to plant trees like rows of corn."[52] Ludwig got his rows of trees, but he probably also caused the extinction of an unknown number of plants, insects, and animals.[53] One author described what it was like to walk through one of the new forests at Jari: "no snakes lurked beneath the log, no birds sang in the branches, and no insects buzzed in the still air."[54]

Jari is unique because of the large size of the undertaking, but other smaller developments are becoming more and more common in the remaining rain forests in Latin America, Africa, and Southeast Asia. Scientists fear that the extinctions which these developments are causing could be a direct threat to the well-being of human as well as other life on earth.

Many of the species in the tropics have never been studied by scientists. But based on past experience, it is believed that many of these unknown species contain properties which could directly benefit humans. Nearly one-half of the prescription drugs now sold in the USA have a natural component in them.[55] How important some of these drugs can be is illustrated by the example of just one plant from the tropical rain forests, the rosy periwinkle. Drugs are now produced from this plant which achieve 80 percent remission in leukemia and Hodgkin's Disease patients.[56]

Exotic species are vital to the health of modern agriculture. The wild varieties and locally developed strains of a number of major grains grown today have characteristics which are of vital importance to modern seed producers. Seeds are needed with natural resistances to the diseases and pests that constantly threaten modern agriculture. Many farmers today utilize only a relatively few, highly productive, varieties of seeds in any one year. The monocultures that are planted are especially vulnerable to diseases and to pests which have developed resistance to the pesticides being used. An example of how this works was shown in 1970, when 15 percent of the corn crop in the USA was killed by a leaf disease, causing a $2 billion loss to farmers and indirectly to consumers because of higher prices. That year, 70 percent of the corn crop used seeds from only five lines of corn. The disease was finally brought under control with the aid of a new variety of corn which was resistant to the leaf disease. The new corn had genetic materials which originated in Mexico.[57]

Insects from tropical forests can at times prove extremely valuable to American farmers. Citrus growers in the USA saved about $25–$30 million a year with the one-time introduction of three parasitic wasps from the tropics, wasps that reproduced and preyed on the pests attacking the citrus fruit.[58] (The introduction of exotic species by humans for profit, for amusement, or by accident into areas to which they are not native is now recognized as having great potential for harm. Since the new species usually has no natural predators in the new area, it can multiply rapidly, destroying or displacing other desirable animals or plants, such as was the case with the introduction of rabbits in Australia, and starlings and the kudzu plant in the USA.)

Biologists Paul and Anne Ehrlich outline three main ways the trend toward increased extinction of species can be reversed. First, human population control is urgently needed in many parts of the world, since it is excessive population pressure which is leading to the destruction of habitats in many cases. Second, large reserves should be set up, in carefully selected areas around the world, so that species can be preserved in their natural settings. Third, a steady-state (the characteristics of a steady-state society will be examined fully in chapter 7) or sustainable society in the world should be created. The Ehrlichs define a sustainable society as "one dedicated to living with environmental constraints rather than perpetually growing with the hopeless goal of conquering nature."[59]

Paul and Anne Ehrlich call upon the rich nations of the world to reverse their "overdevelopment," and to help the poorer nations preserve the tropical habitats by giving them aid and enacting new international trade policies. The Ehrlichs do not believe that the developing nations can preserve the tropical habitats on their own since their financial needs are so great. What is needed in the world, they feel, is a new awareness that the diversity of life forms on earth is a priceless treasure that all humanity benefits from and that all share a responsibility for helping to preserve.[60]

ENVIRONMENTAL POLITICS

In this final section we shall try to understand what makes environmental politics so controversial. Politics is a passionate business, but why are environmental issues often emotional? Obviously, conflicting interests and values must be involved. The definition of politics which was mentioned in the Preface, and which I am using in this book, states that it involves the making of laws and decisions that everyone must obey in a society. These laws and decisions are directed at settling conflicts which arise among people living together in a community, and at achieving commonly desired goals. As we shall see, environmental politics does deal with very strongly held opposing values and interests. It also represents an effort by a community to achieve some goals – such as clean air and clean water – which cannot be reached individually, but only by the community as a whole.

The political scientists Harold and Margaret Sprout have identified two philosophies which they believe are at the root of most environmental conflicts. They believe that most participants in environmental politics show a tendency toward having one of two very different philosophies or world views: one they call "exploitive," and the other "mutualistic." Here is how they define them:

A[n] . . . exploitive attitude would be one that envisages inert matter, nonhuman species, and even humans as objects to be possessed or manipulated to suit the purposes of the exploiter. In contrast, a . . . mutualistic posture would be one that emphasizes the interrelatedness of things and manifests a preference for cooperation and accommodation rather than conflict and domination.[61]

While conflicting world views are a part of environmental politics, so also is a conflict of basic interests. Economist Lester Thurow believes that environmental politics often involves a conflict between different classes which have very different interests. He sees the environmental movement being supported mainly by upper middle-class people who have gained economic security and now want to improve the quality of their lives further by reducing environmental pollutants. On the opposite side, he sees both lower-income groups and the rich – lower-income people because they see environmental laws making it more difficult for them to find jobs and obtain a better income, and the rich because they can often buy their way out of environmental problems and see pollution laws as making it more difficult for them to increase their wealth even further.[62]

Other conflicting interests are also involved in environmental politics. Anti-pollution laws often make it more difficult and costly to increase energy supplies, extract minerals, and increase jobs by industrial growth. Barry Commoner's Fourth Law of Ecology – There Is No Such Thing As a Free Lunch – means that for every gain there is some cost.[63] There are tradeoffs involved in making the air and water cleaner as there are in making more cars and television sets. Also, the costs of pollution control often increase substantially as you try to make the environment cleaner. The cost required to make a 50 percent reduction in a pollutant is often quite modest, whereas if you try to reduce the pollutant by 95 percent, the cost usually increases dramatically.[64]

Much environmental destruction is extremely difficult for the political system to deal with, since the damage often shows up many years after the polluting action takes place. It is now clear that prevention is much cheaper than trying to clean up the damage after it has occurred, but the nature of politics does not lend itself to long-range planning. Generally, politicians have a rather short-term outlook, as do many business people. Both are judged on their performance in handling immediate problems; this promotes a tendency to take actions which show some immediate result. Such actions further the politician's chances for re-election and the business person's profits or chances for promotion. Yet environmental problems often call for actions before the danger becomes clear. A further complication is the fact that, even after action is taken to reduce a pollutant, because of the inherent delays in the system, the harmful effects of the pollutant do not decrease until a number of years later. Thus, the inclination of the public official – and the business person – is to do nothing and hope that something turns up which will show that the problem was not as bad as feared or that there is a cheaper way to deal with it.

An additional factor in environmental politics is unique to the

USA. The American dream has been one of continuing abundance. For much of the country's history, there has seemed to be an unlimited abundance of many things needed for the good life, such as land, forests, minerals, energy, clean air, and natural beauty. It is a country that seems to offer unlimited opportunities for many to make a better life for themselves, and "better" is usually defined as including more material goods. The setting of limits on consumption and production which environmentalists often promote is certain to cause dismay to many, and it does.

If the above were not enough to make environmental politics very difficult, there is also the fact that the costs in environmental matters are often very difficult to measure. One can calculate the cost of a scrubber on a coal-burning power plant, but how do you measure the cost of a shortened life that occurs if the scrubber is not used? How do you place a dollar figure on the suffering that a person with emphysema experiences, or a miner with brown lung disease, or an asbestos worker with cancer? How do you measure the costs the yet unborn will have to pay if nothing is done now about acid rain? And how do you put a dollar figure on the loss of natural beauty? There is no way you can measure these things in terms of money. Because it is so difficult to weigh the costs in conventional terms of measurement, the costs often were not weighed in the past. There is, of course, also the matter of values – the value individuals place on more material goods, higher incomes, open spaces, and clean air. The resolution of conflicts over values can often be handled only by politics, in a democracy by the community as a whole making decisions through its representatives and then requiring all members of the community to obey them. That such stuff causes controversy and stirs passions should not be surprising. It's hard work.

CONCLUSIONS

Development is more than economic growth: it also includes the social changes which are caused by or accompany economic growth. As this chapter has shown, the increase in the production of goods and services which came with industrialization had, and still has, frightening costs. Poverty was basically wiped out in a number of countries by industrialization – obviously an impressive benefit of the new economic activity. But that activity harmed both people and the environment. Slowly and painfully, people in the developed countries came to realize that economic growth was not enough. Attention had to be paid to its effects on the earth and on people. (If one gets cancer, for example, what good is material wealth?) And an awareness did grow in the industrialized nations, and continues to grow, that the question of how economic growth is affecting the environment needs to be asked and answered. The rich countries are slowly learning that it is cheaper and causes much less suffering to try to reduce the harmful effects of an economic activity at the beginning, when it is planned, than after the damage appears. To do this is not easy and is always imperfect. But an awareness of the need for such effort indicates a greater understanding and moral concern than did the previous widespread attitude which focused only on creating new products and services.

The less developed nations are also slowly realizing that the effects of economic activity on the environment should not be ignored. But here the new awareness is less widespread than in the rich countries. This is understandable, because the reduction of poverty is naturally the first concern people have. It explains why some Third World countries have welcomed polluting industries, such as factories that manufacture asbestos, since jobs today are more important than a vague worry that workers may contract cancer in 20 or 30 years. But also in developing countries, a slowly growing number of people realize that if the economic activity which gives jobs to people harms the environment at the same time, the benefits from that economic activity will be short-lived.

Poverty harms the environment, as we saw for example in the case of deforestation, where poor people searching for land to farm and for fuel are the main cause of the extensive destruction of the remaining tropical rain forests. Economic growth which benefits the majority of people is needed to protect the environment. And a control of the rapidly expanding populations of many of the poorest countries is also needed to protect the environment, since increasing numbers of poor people hurt the land on which they live as they struggle to survive.

For both rich and poor nations, the environment is important. Economic growth is also important, especially for the poorer countries. The challenge remains for both poor and rich to achieve a balance between economic activity and a protection of the land, air, and water upon which life depends.

442.

NOTES

1 Steve Van Matre and Bill Weiler (eds), *The Earth Speaks* (Warrenville, Ill: Institute for Earth Education, 1983), p. 122.
2 Erik P. Eckholm, *Down to Earth* (New York: W. W. Norton, 1982), p. 95.
3 Lester Brown, *The Twenty-ninth Day* (New York: W. W. Norton, 1978), p. 44. One of the ways Britain reduced its air pollution – by building tall smokestacks – has probably led to worse air in Scandinavia.
4 *Environmental Quality 1982: 13th Annual Report of The Council on Environmental Quality* (Washington, DC: US Government Printing Office, 1982), p. 24.
5 *The New York Times*, late city edn (September 23, 1980), p. A2.
6 *The New York Times*, late city edn (May 13, 1980), p. C3.
7 *The New York Times*, late edn (May 20, 1982, p. A15; September 2, 1982, p. A13).
8 *The New York Times*, late edn (June 9, 1983), p. A17.
9 Barry Commoner, *The Closing Circle* (New York: Alfred Knopf, 1971), p. 39.
10 *The New York Times*, late edn (June 30, 1983), p. A16.
11 Eckholm, *Down to Earth*, p. 126.
12 *The New York Times*, late edn (March 28, 1983), p. 1.
13 Brown, *The Twenty-ninth Day*, p. 40.
14 *Christian Scientist Monitor* (May 30, 1984), p. 1.
15 Peter Stoler, "Is Clean Water a Thing of the Past?" *Sierra* (March/April 1981), p. 15.
16 Ibid., p. 14.
17 Dennis Drabelle, "Exploring Water Problems," *Sierra* (May/June 1983), p. 99.
18 Joyce Egginton, "The Long Island Lesson," *Audubon*, 83 (July 1981), p. 89.
19 Council on Environmental Quality and the Department of State, *The Global 2000 Report to the President*, vol. 1 (New York: Penguin Books, 1982), p. 26.
20 Jorgen Randers and Dennis Meadows, "The Dynamics of Solid

Waste Generation," in Dennis and Donella Meadows (eds), *Toward Global Equilibrium* (Cambridge, Mass.: Wright-Allen Press, 1973), p. 167.

21 See Adeline Levine, *Love Canal: Science, Politics and People* (Lexington, Mass.: Lexington Books, 1982) and Michael Brown, *Laying Waste: The Poisoning of America by Toxic Wastes* (New York: Pantheon Books, 1980).

22 Totals may vary depending on the definition used of toxic wastes and the agency doing the estimates: *The New York Times*, late edn (March 17, 1983, p. B14; April 28, 1984, p. 9).

23 Levine, *Love Canal*, p. 218.

24 James Aucoin, "Dioxin in Missouri: The Search Continues for a Cleanup Strategy," *Sierra* (January–February 1984), pp. 22–6.

25 *The New York Times*, late edn (March 11, 1985), p. D12.

26 Barbara Ward, *Progress for a Small Planet* (New York: W. W. Norton, 1979), pp. 65–6.

27 Mary Durant, "Here We Go A-Bottling, *Audubon*, 88 (May 1986), p. 32.

28 Michael Royston, "Making Pollution Prevention Pay," *Harvard Business Review* (November–December 1980), p. 12.

29 Sandra Postel, "Protecting Forests," in Lester Brown (ed.), *State of the World* (New York: W. W. Norton, 1984), p. 74.

30 *The New York Times*, late edn (July 5, 1983), p. C1.

31 Norman Myers, *The Primary Source* (New York: W. W. Norton, 1984), p. 143.

32 Anne LaBastille, "Heaven, Not Hell," *Audubon*, 81 (November 1979), p. 91.

33 *The New York Times*, late edn (January 24, 1984), p. C2.

34 Christopher Uhl, "You Can Keep a Good Forest Down," *Natural History*, 92 (April 1983), p. 78.

35 Brown, *The Twenty-ninth Day*, p. 57.

36 Richard Peto, "Why Cancer?" in Julian Simon and Herman Kahn (eds) *The Resourceful Earth*, (Oxford, England: Basil Blackwell, 1984), pp. 528–44; *The New York Times*, late edn (March 20, 1984), p. C1.

37 David Weir and Mark Schapiro, *Circle of Poison* (San Francisco: Institute for Food and Development Policy, 1981), p. 4.

38 Martin Wolterding, "The Poisoning of Central America," *Sierra* (September–October 1981), p. 63.

39 Ibid., p. 64.

40 Weir and Schapiro, *Circle of Poison*, p. 28.

41 *The New York Times*, late edn (April 21, 1986), p. A14.

42 *The New York Times*, late edn (March 3, 1984), p. 10.

43 Commoner, *The Closing Circle*, p. 261.

44 Hans Landsberg, et al., "Nonfuel Minerals," in Paul Portney (ed.), *Current Issues in Natural Resource Policy* (Washington, DC: Resources for the Future, 1982), p. 82.

45 Ibid., p. 83.

46 Dennis Pirages, *The New Context for International Relations: Global Ecopolitics* (North Scituate, Mass.: Duxbury Press, 1978), p. 172.

47 Brown, *The Twenty-ninth Day*, p. 284.

48 Jeremy Rifkin, *Entropy* (New York: Viking Press, 1980), p. 117.

49 Brown, *The Twenty-ninth Day*, p. 284.

50 Charles Birch, *Confronting the Future* (New York: Penguin, 1976), p. 35.

51 Norman Myers, "The Exhausted Earth," *Foreign Policy*, 42 (Spring 1981), p. 141.

52 Loren McIntyre, "Jari: A Billion Dollar Gamble," *National Geographic* (May 1980), p. 701.

53 After 14 years of building Jari, Ludwig abandoned the project in 1982 and sold it to Brazilians for a loss.

54 McIntryre, "Jari," p. 711.

55 Peter Raven, "Tropical Rain Forests: A Global Responsibility," *Natural History*, 90 (February 1981), p. 29.

56 Myers, "The Exhausted Earth," p. 145.

57 Ibid., p. 143.

58 Norman Myers, "Room in the Ark?" *Bulletin of the Atomic Scientists*, 38 (November 1982), p. 48.

59 Paul R. Ehrlich and Anne H. Ehrlich, *Extinction* (New York: Random House, 1981), pp. 242–3.

60 Ibid., especially ch. 10. Note their following statement: "over 95 percent of the organisms capable of competing seriously with humanity for food or of doing us harm by transmitting diseases are now controlled gratis by other species in natural ecosystems" (p. 94).

61 Harold Sprout and Margaret Sprout, *The Context of Environmental Politics* (Lexington, Ky.: University Press of Kentucky, 1978), pp. 47–8.

62 Lester Thurow, *The Zero-sum Society* (New York: Basic Books, 1980), pp. 104–5.

63 Commoner, *The Closing Circle*, pp. 45–6.

64 William Ophuls, *Ecology and the Politics of Scarcity* (San Francisco: W. H. Freeman, 1977), p. 75.

6

Technology and Development

> The unleashed power of the atom has changed everything save our modes of thinking, and we thus drift toward unparalleled catastrophes.
>
> Albert Einstein (1879–1955)

To many people, technology and development are synonymous. Technology is what makes economic growth and social change happen. The use of advanced technology is what makes "modern" societies modern. The less modern societies – the non-Western, less developed, poor nations – use much less advanced technology. To many, the limited use of high technology by the less developed nations is one of the main reasons why they are less developed and less prosperous than the Western industrialized nations. But the relationship between technology and development is a complicated one. At times the negative features of technology seem to outweigh the positive features. Technology can cause a society to change in some very undesirable ways. In this chapter we will look closely at some of the negative relationships between technology and development and at some of the main political issues which arise from these relationships.

BENEFITS OF TECHNOLOGY

A book such as this one, whose readers will probably be mostly from the developed nations, does not need to dwell on the benefits of technology. Advertising and the mass media herald the expected joys which will come with the new product, technique, or discovery. In the USA we are socialized to like new things; the American reputation for being a pragmatic people means that science and its application, technology, are commonly used to solve problems, to make things work "better." One would have to be a fool not to recognize the benefits that technology has brought. In personal terms, it has allowed me to visit about 40 countries; to see a photograph of the earth taken from space; to write this book on a personal computer which greatly facilitated its composition; to wear shirts that don't need ironing; and to keep my glaucoma under control so that I do not go blind.

One of the main reasons much of the world envies the USA is not only because it is rich, but because its technology has in many real ways made life more comfortable, stimulating, and free of drudgery. We Americans know this and need to remember it. But we also need to learn several other lessons: (1) short-term benefits from using a technology can make it impossible for us to achieve some long-term goals; (2) there can be unanticipated consequences of using a technology; (3) the use of some types of technology in certain situations can be inappropriate; and (4) there are many problems which technology cannot solve. The inability to learn these lessons could lead to our destruction, as the case study in this chapter on the threat of nuclear war will show.

SHORT-TERM VERSUS LONG-TERM BENEFITS

Garrett Hardin, a biologist, has coined the phrase "the tragedy of the commons" to describe what can happen when short-term interests and long-term interests of people are in conflict.[1] Hardin shows how it is rational and in the best short-term interest of each herdsman in a village to increase the number of cattle he has grazing on the "commons," the commonly owned lands in the village. The benefit to an individual herdsman of increasing the number of cattle he has there is greater than the harm which comes from the overgrazing which the additional cattle create; the cost of the overgrazing will be shared by all the herdsmen using the commons, while the individual herdsman will reap the profit which comes from selling additional cattle. Also, if the individual herdsman does not increase his cattle but others increase theirs, he loses out since the overgrazing harms his cattle. Thus, the tragedy occurs. Each herdsman, acting rationally and in his own best short-term interest, increases his stock on the commons. Soon there is so much overgrazing that the grass dies and then the cattle die.

The global commons today are those parts of the planet which are used by many or all nations: the oceans, the international river systems, the seabed, the atmosphere, and outer space. Technology can give some nations an advantage over others in exploiting this commons and it is clearly in their short-term interest to do so. So it is with commercial fishing in the world's oceans. Technology has made possible bigger and more powerful fishing boats, equipped with sonar to locate schools of fish. This technology was mainly responsible for the steadily increasing catches of fish world-wide up until the late 1960s, when they peaked and then started to decline. There is every indication that many species of fish are being "overgrazed," and if this is not controlled, all nations which use the oceans for fishing will be hurt. Not only will their fishing industries be hurt, but unique forms of life on earth will probably become extinct. Such could well be the fate of many species of the fish-like mammal, the whale, unless recent international efforts to drastically reduce the numbers of whales killed succeed in allowing whale populations to increase.

An example of technology giving a nation advantages over others in exploiting the global commons can be seen in the history of the Law of the Seas Treaty, which governs the use and exploitation of the seas. This treaty, which took eight years to negotiate, was approved in 1982 by 130 nations at the United Nations. The USA was one of four nations to vote against it. One of the reasons for its opposition was that it was unwilling to share its advanced sea mining technology with a global mining authority. The short-term advantages to the USA of not sharing its mining technology are clear, but these advantages conflict with long-term interests of the USA and other nations in having a peaceful and mutually agreed upon arrangement for the use of this part of the global commons. Donald Puchala summarizes the matter well:

> The United States would probably benefit from a short-run scramble to close off the commons and parcel it into national jurisdictions. Since our technology permits us to exploit now

what others can only hope to exploit in the future, we would for a time command the lion's share of the parcelled commons. But there should be no doubt that such a policy would invite challenge and conflict in the future . . .[2]

Another example of a "tragedy of the commons" situation is pollution. An individual gains a short-term advantage by polluting – for example, by disconnecting the pollution control device on his or her car to decrease gasoline consumption (some of my students confess to doing this) – but the long-term interests of the whole community are hurt by the polluting of the air. In fact, the lungs of the individual doing the polluting may be hurt in the long run by his or her auto's pollution. While this is true, the attractiveness of the short-term benefit over the long-term interests for any one individual can be overwhelming. Such was the case when I bought my 1979 car. I had a choice of buying a 1979 model which used leaded gasoline, or a 1980 model which used unleaded gasoline. Although I knew in a general way at that time that using unleaded gasoline was better for the environment, I bought the 1979 model because leaded gasoline was cheaper.

The way out of this situation in which individuals gain benefits from polluting calls for a political solution – one designed by the community or its representatives, and which all members of the community will have to obey. In the example involving my students, a possible solution would be more effective auto inspections and the use of steep fines for removing the pollution control device. In the example involving me, a simple solution would have been for the government to place a higher tax on leaded gasoline than on non-leaded to equalize their price so that there would not have been a monetary advantage for me to pick the 1979 model over the 1980 model.

The exporting of nuclear technology is also likely to be a "tragedy of the commons" situation. Nuclear reprocessing plants and uranium enrichment plants produce plutonium and uranium which can be used for making nuclear weapons. The USA, West Germany, and France have competed with each other to sell Third World countries nuclear reactors and nuclear technologies. The Soviet Union has a much better record in this area than Western nations as it has been very reluctant to export its nuclear technology. The fact that many of the Third World nations that are getting nuclear technology are politically unstable and involved in heated regional conflicts makes this potential "tragedy of the commons" situation very dangerous indeed. As more nations acquire nuclear weapons, the odds go up that they will be used. And the danger that a local conflict will draw in the superpowers is real.[3]

UNANTICIPATED CONSEQUENCES OF THE USE OF TECHNOLOGY

Ecology is the study of the relationships between organisms and their environments. Without a knowledge of ecology, one is tempted to use technology to solve a single problem. But there are many examples to illustrate the truth that one can't change one part of the human environment without in some way affecting other parts. Often these other effects are harmful, and often they are completely unanticipated.[4] Take for example the following situation which occurred in Borneo. There, the efforts of health officials to destroy malaria-carrying mosquitoes by spraying houses with DDT led to the collapsing of the roofs of village houses and to the need to parachute cats into the villages:

> [S]hortly [after the spraying] the roofs of the natives' houses began to fall because they were being eaten by caterpillars, which, because of their particular habits, had not absorbed very much of the DDT themselves. A certain predatory wasp, however, which had been keeping the caterpillars under control, had been killed off in large numbers by the DDT. But the story doesn't end here, because they brought the spraying indoors to control houseflies. Up to that time, the control of houseflies was largely the job of a little lizard, the gecko, that inhabits houses. Well, the geckos continued their job of eating flies, now heavily dosed with DDT, and the geckos began to die. Then the geckos were eaten by house cats. The poor house cats at the end of this food chain had concentrated this material, and they began to die. And they died in such numbers that rats began to invade the houses and consume the

food. But, more important, the rats were potential plague carriers. This situation became so alarming that they finally resorted to parachuting fresh cats into Borneo to try to restore the balance of populations that the people, trigger-happy with the spray guns, had destroyed.[5]

The use of DDT in the USA also had awesome unanticipated effects since it is persistent (it does not easily break down into harmless substances) and is poisonous to many forms of life.[6] According to one study, many of the effects of the use of DDT could not have been predicted before its use.[7] The author of this study believes that only through the close monitoring of the effects of new chemicals and through an open debate on those effects can chemicals such as DDT be controlled.

Let's look at factory farms and the unanticipated consequences that have come with the adoption of factory techniques to produce animals for human consumption. Such techniques have been adopted to raise poultry, pigs, veal calves, and cattle. The techniques allow large numbers of animals to be raised in a relatively small space. (Many of these animals never see the light of day until they are removed for slaughter.) The crowding of many animals in a small space and the confinement of individual animals in small stalls creates stress, frustration, and boredom in the animals. Stress can lower the natural defenses of the animals to diseases, and the crowded conditions facilitate the rapid spreading of diseases among the animals. It is common for factory-raised animals to receive large doses of antibiotics in their feed to prevent the outbreak of such diseases. There is now evidence that the abundant use of antibiotics in animal food is creating bacteria which are resistant to treatment by modern drugs and that these bacteria can cause illness in humans.[8] Large amounts of other drugs (to promote rapid growth, for example) and pesticides (to control the highly unsanitary conditions caused by many animals being kept in a small space) are showing up in the meat and poultry coming out of the factory farms. A Department of Agriculture study undertaken between 1974 and 1976 showed that about 15 percent of the meat and poultry it sampled had illegally high levels of drugs and pesticides.[9]

The Green Revolution had unanticipated negative consequences along with its success in raising grain production in the Third World. In parts of India where the land was relatively evenly distributed before the Green Revolution, the new farming techniques worked well to increase both production and rural employment. But in other parts of the world where the ownership of the land was highly uneven, with a few large landowners and many small ones – a common situation in the Third World – the Green Revolution caused the few rich farmers to get richer and the many poor farmers to get poorer. Here is why that happened:

Large farmers generally adopt the new methods first. They have the capital to do so and can afford to take the risk. Although the new seed varieties do not require tractor mechanization, they provide much economic incentive for mechanization, especially where multiple cropping requires a quick harvest and replanting. On large farms, simple economic considerations lead almost inevitably to the use of labor-displacing machinery and to the purchase of still more land. The ultimate effects of this . . . are agricultural unemployment, increased migration to the city, and perhaps even increased malnutrition, since the poor and unemployed do not have the means to buy the newly produced food.[10]

The unanticipated consequences of the use of technology can be seen in a situation of which I have some personal knowledge. When I was in Iran in the late 1950s with the US foreign aid program, one of our projects was to modernize the police force of the monarch, the Shah of Iran. We gave the national police new communications equipment so that police messages could be sent throughout the country quickly and efficiently. The USA gave such assistance to the Shah to bolster his regime and help him to maintain public order in Iran while development programs were being initiated. All fine and good, except for the fact that the Shah used his now efficient police – and especially his secret police, which the US CIA helped train – not just to catch criminals and those who were trying to violently overthrow his government, but to suppress all opponents of his regime. His secret police, SAVAK, soon earned a world-wide reputation for being very efficient – and ruthless. Their ruthlessness, which often involved torturing suspected opponents of the Shah, was one of the reasons why the Shah became very unpopular in Iran and was eventually overthrown in 1979 by the Ayatollah Khomeini, a person who had deep anti-American feelings.[11]

INAPPROPRIATE USES OF TECHNOLOGY

In 1973, E. F. Schumacher published his book *Small is Beautiful: Economics As If People Mattered.*[12] This book became the foundation for a movement which seeks to use technology in ways that are not harmful to people. Schumacher argued that the developing nations need intermediate (or "appropriate") technology, not the high (or "hard") technology of the Western industrialized nations. Intermediate technology lies in between the ineffective and primitive technology which is common in the rural areas of the Third World – where most of the world's people live – and the technology of the industrialized world, which tends to use vast amounts of energy, pollutes the environment, requires imported resources, and often alienates the workers from their own work. The intermediate technology movement seeks to identify those areas of life in the Third World, and also in the industrialized West, where a relatively simple technology can make people's work easier but also meaningful, that is, can give them a feeling of satisfaction when they do it.

It is the lack of this satisfaction, or contentment, which is often absent in workers in developed nations. A good example of this can be seen in the "workers' revolt" which took place in the ultramodern automobile plant in Lordstown, Ohio, which was to produce Vegas for General Motors and which incorporated the latest in automated technology. The revolt led to a vote by 97 percent of the workers to strike over working conditions. The workers' discontent with the new plant and its mass production techniques can be summed up by the suggestion of one of the strikers that the workers ought to take a sign which was attached to some of the machines, "Treat Me with Respect and I will give you Top Quality Work with Less Effort," and print it on their T-shirts.[13]

The high technology of the West is often very expensive, and thus large amounts of capital are needed to acquire it, capital which most Third World nations do not have. This technology is referred to as being capital-intensive instead of labor-intensive. This means that money is needed to obtain it and maintain it – but not many people. In other words, high technology does not give many workers jobs. (This is the essence of the mass production line – lots of products by a relatively small number of workers.) But the main problem in nations that are trying to develop – and, in fact, in the USA also when its economy is in a recession – is that there are not enough jobs for people in the first place. It is the absence of jobs in the rural areas that is causing large numbers of the rural poor in the Third World to migrate to the cities looking for work, work that is often not there.

I have witnessed the inappropriate use of high technology in both Liberia and the USA. As part of the US economic assistance to Liberia, we gave the Liberians road-building equipment. That equipment included power saws. As I proceeded to turn some of this equipment over to Liberians in a small town in a rural area, I realized that the power saws we were giving them were very inappropriate. To people who had little or no experience with power tools – which applied to nearly all the Liberians in that town – the power saw was a deadly instrument. Also, they would not be able to maintain them or repair them when they broke down. Their noise would ruin the peacefulness of the area. A much more appropriate form of assistance would have been crates of axes and hand saws, tools they could easily learn to use safely, and would be able to maintain and repair themselves; these would have provided work for many people.

In the USA I became aware of the inappropriate use of high technology as my wife and I began to prepare for the birth of our children. Most children in the world are born at home, but in the USA and in many other developed countries nearly all births take place in hospitals. An impressive number of studies now show that moving births into hospitals has resulted in unnecessary interventions in the birth process by doctors and hospital staff which upset the natural stages of labor and can jeopardize the health of both the mother and the baby.[14] As many as 85–90 percent of women can give birth naturally, without the use of technology being required.[15] Prenatal care can usually identify the 10–15 percent that can't deliver normally, and for them the use of technology can help protect the lives of the mother and baby. But the major error that has been made is that procedures that are appropriate for these few are now routinely used for most births.

The intermediate technology movement is not against high technology as such (it recognizes areas where high technology is desirable – there is no other way to produce vaccines against deadly diseases, for example) but only against the use of such technology where simpler technology would be appropriate.

LIMITS TO THE "TECHNOLOGICAL FIX"

In our society, which makes wide use of technology, there is a common belief that technology can solve our most urgent problems. It is even believed that the problems that science and technology have created can be solved by more science and technology. What is lacking, according to this way of thinking, is better use of science and technology to solve the problem at hand, or, to find a "technological fix."

While the ability of technology to solve certain problems is impressive, there are a number of serious problems confronting humans – in fact, probably the most serious problems which humans have ever faced – which seem to have no technological solution. Technology itself has often played a major role in causing these problems. Let's look at a few of them.

The population explosion appears to have no acceptable technological solution. Birth control devices can certainly help in controlling population growth; without such devices a solution to the problem would be even more difficult than it is. But as we have seen in the chapter on population, the reasons for the population explosion are much more complicated than the lack of birth control devices. Economic, social, and political factors play a significant role in this situation and must be taken into consideration in any effort to control the explosion. A technological advancement which was one of the causes of the population explosion – the wiping out of major diseases, such as smallpox, which used to kill millions – cannot be utilized in the solution. One cannot advocate worse medical care for people to solve the population problem. One must look to other measures for a solution. Some people, such as Garret

Hardin, have argued that many of those people who are advocating technological solutions to the population problem such as farming the seas, developing new strains of wheat, or creating space colonies, "are trying to find a way to avoid the evils of over-population without relinquishing any of the privileges they now enjoy."[16]

Huge municipal sanitation plants were once considered the answer to our polluted streams, rivers, and lakes, but the rising costs of these plants and their only partial effectiveness are bringing this solution into question.[17] As much water pollution is caused by agricultural and urban runoff as by sewage. To talk about a technological fix for this problem is to talk about spending astronomical sums of money, and even then the solution would still be in doubt.

A final example will be given to illustrate the limits to the technological fix. As we shall see in the case study below, the nuclear arms race threatens the world with a holocaust beyond comprehension. Many believe that technology will solve this problem; all we need to gain security are better and more weapons than the Soviets. But the history of the arms race since World War II clearly shows that one side's advantage has been soon matched or surpassed by new weapons by the other side. Momentary feelings of security by one nation have been soon replaced by deepening insecurity felt by both nations as the weapons became more lethal. The "security dilemma" is the phrase which has been coined to describe a situation where one nation's efforts to gain security lead to its opponent's feeling of insecurity. This insecurity causes the nation that believes it is behind in the arms race to build up its arms; but this causes the other nation now to feel insecure. So the race goes on. The temptation to believe that a new weapon will solve the problem is immense. A brief history of the arms race shows how both superpowers have been caught in a security dilemma.

The USA exploded its first atomic bomb in 1945 and felt fairly secure until the Soviets exploded one in 1949. In 1954 the USA tested the first operational thermonuclear weapon (a hydrogen or H-bomb), which uses the A-bomb as a trigger, and a year later the Soviets followed suit. In 1957 the Soviets successfully tested the first intercontinental ballistic missile (ICBM) and put up the earth's first artificial satellite, Sputnik, in the same year. The USA felt very insecure, but within three years had more operational ICBMs than the Soviet Union.[18]

The Soviet Union put up the first anti-ballistic missile system around a city – Moscow – in the 1960s, and in 1968 the USA countered with developing MIRVs (multiple, independently targetable re-entry vehicles), which can easily overwhelm the Soviet anti-ballistic missiles. The Soviets started deploying their first MIRVs in 1975, and these highly accurate missiles with as many as ten warheads on a single missile, each one able to hit a different target, led President Reagan in 1981 to declare that a "window of vulnerability" exists, since the land-based US ICBMs can now be attacked by the Soviet MIRVs. Reagan called for a massive military build-up, and the Soviets stated that they would match any US build-up.

The technological race is now moving into space, with President Reagan in 1983 announcing plans to develop a defensive system, some of which would probably be based in space, which could attack any Soviet missiles fired at the USA. The Soviets have stated that if the USA develops such a system (formally known as the Strategic Defense Initiative, and informally called "Star Wars"), they might increase their missiles so they can overwhelm it or develop other countermeasures to block its effectiveness.

THE THREAT OF NUCLEAR WAR: A CASE STUDY

The threat of nuclear war is a subject which touches on many of the themes we have examined in this chapter. It is the "ultimate" politics of development subject since it is the achievements of weapons technology by the developed nations that has brought the survival of human life into question. It is a problem that cries out for a political solution. Karl von Clausewitz, the famous Prussian author of books on military strategy, described war as a continuation of politics by other means. But, given the probable consequences of a nuclear war as presented below, one must ask whether war between nations with nuclear weapons can remain a way of settling their disputes, or whether they should create a new way to settle political conflicts. Let us look first at the nature of the threat that nuclear weapons have created and then at the main political choices we have for dealing with that threat.

The Threat

It has taken 4½ billion years for life to reach its present state of development on this planet. The year 1945 represents a milestone in that evolution since it was then that the USA exploded its first atomic bombs on Hiroshima and Nagasaki and demonstrated that humans had learned how to harness for war the essential forces of the universe. From 1945, when the USA had no more than two or three atomic bombs, we have now reached a point where the two superpowers, the USA and the USSR, have a total of about 50,000 nuclear weapons, the equivalent of 1 million Hiroshima bombs – or, to put it another way, about 3 tons of TNT for every man, woman, and child in the world. The Hiroshima bomb was a 15 kiloton device (a kiloton has the explosive force of 1,000 tons of TNT): some of the weapons today fall in the megaton range (a megaton is the equivalent of 1 million tons of TNT[19]). In addition to the USA and the Soviet Union, Britain, France, and China have nuclear weapons which could be used in a nuclear war.

What would happen if these weapons are ever used? We can't be sure of all the effects, of course, since, as the author Jonathan Schell has stated, we have only one earth and can't experiment with it.[20] But we do know from the Hiroshima and Nagasaki bombings, and from the numerous testings of nuclear weapons both above and below ground, that there are five immediate destructive effects from a nuclear explosion: (1) the initial radiation, mainly gamma rays; (2) an electromagnetic pulse which, in a high-altitude explosion, can knock out electrical equipment over a very large area; (3) a thermal pulse which consists of bright light (you would be blinded by glancing at the fireball even if you were many miles away) and intense heat (equal to that at the center of the Sun); (4) a blast wave that can flatten buildings; and (5) radioactive fallout, mainly in dirt and debris which is sucked up into the mushroom cloud and then falls to earth.

The longer-term effects from a nuclear explosion are three: (1) delayed or world-wide fallout, which gradually over months and even years falls to the ground, often in rain; (2) a change in the climate (possibly a drastic lowering of the earth's temperature over the whole Northern Hemisphere, which could ruin agricultural crops and cause widespread famine); and (3) a partial destruction of the ozone layer, the layer which protects the earth from the sun's harmful ultraviolet rays. If the ozone layer is depleted, unprotected Caucasians could stay outdoors for only about ten minutes before getting an incapacitating sunburn (blacks, because of the color of their skin, could go somewhat longer), and people would suffer a type of snowblindness from the rays which, if repeated, would lead to permanent blindness. Many animals would suffer the same fate.[21]

Civil defense measures might save some people in a limited nuclear war but would not help much if there were a full-scale nuclear war.[22] Underground shelters in cities hit by nuclear weapons would be turned into ovens since they would tend to concentrate the heat released from the blast and the firestorms. Nor does an evacuation of the cities look like a hopeful remedy in a full-scale nuclear war, since people would not be protected from fallout, or from re-targeted missiles, and could not survive well in an economy which had collapsed.

Since most of our hospitals and many doctors are in central-city areas and would be hit by the first missiles in an all-out nuclear war, medical care would not be available for the millions of people suffering from burns, puncture wounds, shock, and radiation sickness. Many corpses would remain unburied and would create a serious health hazard, which would contribute to the danger of epidemics spreading among the population whose resistance to disease had been lowered by radiation exposure, malnutrition, and shock.

What could be the final result of all this? Here is how Jonathan Schell answers that question in probably the longest sentence you have ever read, but in one with no wasted words:

> Bearing in mind that the possible consequences of the detonations of thousands of megatons of nuclear explosives include the blinding of insects, birds, and beasts all over the world; the extinction of many ocean species, among them some at the base of the food chain; the temporary or permanent alteration of the climate of the globe, with the

outside chance of "dramatic" and "major" alterations in the structure of the atmosphere; the pollution of the whole ecosphere with oxides of nitrogen; the incapacitation in ten minutes of unprotected people who go out into the sunlight; the blinding of people who go out into the sunlight; a significant decrease in photosynthesis in plants around the world; the scalding and killing of many crops; the increase in rates of cancer and mutation around the world, but especially in the targeted zones, and the attendant risk of global epidemics; the possible poisoning of all vertebrates by sharply increased levels of vitamin D in their skin as a result of increased ultraviolet light; and the outright slaughter on all targeted continents of most human beings and other living things by the initial nuclear radiation, the fireballs, the thermal pulses, the blast waves, the mass fires, and the fallout from the explosions; and considering that these consequences will all interact with one another in unguessable ways and, furthermore, are in all likelihood an incomplete list, which will be added to as our knowledge of the earth increases, one must conclude that a full-scale nuclear holocaust could lead to the extinction of mankind.[23]

The Choices

There are two basic political choices concerning how to deal with the threat of nuclear war: arm or disarm. The advocates of each choice argue that theirs is the best way to prevent a nuclear war. Since both can't be right – one way is bound to make nuclear war more likely – it is of the utmost importance that we know the main arguments of each side and evaluate the strengths and weaknesses of each position.

Arm According to this position, the USA is forced to increase its nuclear armaments because the Soviet Union is superior to the USA in the overall number of vehicles which can deliver nuclear weapons (especially in land-based missiles and submarines), in medium-range missiles targeted on Europe, and in total explosive power of its nuclear force. The Soviets spend a higher portion of their GNP on defense than the USA does. Also, the Soviet Union has a superiority over the USA in conventional military forces in Europe, especially tanks; American nuclear weapons are needed to deter the Soviets from using that superiority to threaten Europe or vital oil interests in the Persian Gulf area. The USA must retain the right to use nuclear weapons first in a war with the Soviet Union because the Soviets need to know that, if they invade Europe, or the Persian Gulf area, the USA will use its tactical (battlefield) nuclear weapons to stop the Soviet advance. It is this US policy which prevents Soviet aggression.

The USSR has developed an ability to fight a protracted nuclear war, so the USA must acquire the same ability in order to convince the Soviets that they cannot win such a war. If the Soviets are so convinced, they will not attack the USA or its allies.

The Soviets are an expansionist power, and even if they don't start a war with their superior arms, they will use their superiority to blackmail the USA into agreeing to various demands. An American arms build-up, therefore, will prevent Soviet adventurism, an attempt to gain advantages in the Third World and in other areas in which the USA has vital interests.

In·order to keep intact the policy of deterrence (the ability to retaliate and destroy your enemy even if he attacks you first), improvements must be made in a number of American weapons. New airplanes must be developed which will have increased ability to get through improved Soviet air defenses, the American Navy must keep its lead over the Soviets in anti-submarine technology, and our land-based missiles, which are now vulnerable to attack by new, accurate Soviet missiles, must be made invulnerable again.

The USA military build-up will force the Soviets to participate in meaningful arms control talks. The economy of the Soviet Union is weak, and if they don't agree to a limit on arms the USA will create serious strains on their economy as they try to match its build-up.

Deterrence may not be able to preserve the peace forever: it could fail. Efforts must be placed on developing a defensive system which could protect the USA from attacking missiles. Although it is not yet known whether such a defense can be created, the USA should try. No matter what the Strategic Defense Initiative/Star Wars system costs, it would be well worth the funds spent on it.

The Soviet Union is a totalitarian country, a country that has used brutal repression against its own people and against people it gains contol over, such as Afghanistan which it invaded in 1979 and indirectly in Poland in 1981. It is a country that cannot be trusted and one that only respects strength in its opponents. American superiority in nuclear arms has kept the peace for the past three decades; thus, the USA should do everything necessary to regain that superiority.

Disarm According to this position, now is the right time to press for disarmament. The USA and USSR are roughly equal in strategic forces (forces that can hit each other's homeland). In fact, the USA is ahead of the Soviet Union in numbers of nuclear warheads and bombs, and has always been ahead of it in this measure of strength. Because of a rough parity now, both sides could agree to disarmament without being frozen into a position of inferiority, something neither side would agree to.

If the arms race continues, the chances for a nuclear war increase greatly. The new weapons that are being developed now or are actually being deployed are counterforce or first-strike weapons; that is, they are very accurate and can be used to attack the other side's missiles and command centers. When many of these weapons are in place on both sides, a crisis involving the two superpowers could easily cause one of them to attack the other for fear that the other side was planning to attack. It is in fact likely that the Soviet Union would do this, since most of its nuclear weapons are vulnerable land-based missiles whereas most of the US nuclear warheads are on relatively invulnerable submarines. The dominating thought in such a crisis would probably be "launch them or lose them." When many counterforce weapons are deployed, one or both of the superpowers will probably adopt a "launch on warning" system (you launch your missiles when your computers indicate that enemy missiles are heading toward yours). This would be very dangerous for the world because an accident could start the war. Computer mistakes are not uncommon: in 1979 a US computer accidentally read a tape used for testing the system as being an actual Soviet attack, and in 1980 a 46-cent silicone chip malfunctioned in a US computer, causing the computer to report that the USSR had launched missiles against the USA.

Superiority of nuclear weapons has become meaningless. Neither side can stop the other side's missiles from reaching their targets once launched, so there will be no winner in a nuclear war: both sides will lose. Superiority of arms did make sense in past wars, where one side could win and one lose, but nuclear weapons have changed this.

The arms race is very expensive; one submarine now costs over $1 billion; the Star Wars system could cost up to $1 trillion. Both the USA and the USSR have serious social needs for which they could use these funds.

The Star Wars idea represents another example of misplaced faith in technology. No missile defensive system could stop all attacking missiles from reaching their targets. Even if only a few get through, they would be enough to destroy the USA or the Soviet Union as modern societies.

Where will the choice of arms build-up lead? It will lead to a move into space with anti-satellite weapons and military space stations. Each spiral of the arms race makes the world we live in more dangerous and both sides more fearful and suspicious. The present time is in some ways like the period just before World War I when an arms build-up and opposing military alliances helped lead to a war which no country wanted, a war which turned out to be much bloodier than anyone had anticipated.

CONCLUSIONS

This chapter has focused on the negative aspects of technology. It has done so because most of the readers of this book will probably be citizens of developed countries who already have a strong belief in the advantages of technology. It is not my intent to undermine that belief, because technology has benefited human beings in countless ways, and its use is largely responsible for the high living standards in the USA and other industrialized nations. Rather, my intent is to bring a healthy caution to the use of technology. An ignoring of the negative potential of technology has brought harm to people in the past and could cause unprecedented harm in the future. Technology is basically neutral. Most of it is neither good nor bad. It is the use that human beings make of technology that determines whether it is mainly beneficial or harmful.

The less developed nations need technology to help them solve many of their awesome problems. But often intermediate technology should be used by them rather than the high technology of the industrialized nations. The temptation to imitate the West is strong, but ample evidence exists to show that this could be a serious mistake for developing nations. The Third World needs to remember that its conditions and needs are different from those of the West, and that it should take from Western science only what is appropriate.

The industrial nations face another task. They must become more discriminating in their use of technology and lose some of their fascination with and childlike faith in technology. The fate of the earth is now literally in their hands, especially in the hands of the USA and the USSR. The wisdom or lack of wisdom they show in using military technology affects all – the present inhabitants of earth, both human and non-human, and future generations, who depend on our good judgment for their chance to experience life on this planet.

NOTES

1 Garrett Hardin, "The Tragedy of the Commons," *Science*, 162 (December 13, 1968), pp. 1243–8.
2 Donald J. Puchala, "American Interests and the United Nations," *Political Science Quarterly*, 97 (Winter 1982–3), p. 585.
3 See Nigel Calder, *Nuclear Nightmares: An Investigation Into Possible Wars* (New York: Penguin Books, 1979), ch. 3, "The Nuclear Epidemic," on how this can happen.
4 A description of 50 case studies of development projects in the Third World which had harmful and unanticipated effects on the environment is contained in the following conference report: M. Taghi Farvar and John P. Milton (eds), *The Careless Technology: Ecology and International Development* (Garden City, NY: Natural History Press, 1972).
5 "Ecology: The New Great Chain of Being," *Natural History*, 77 (December 1968), p. 8.
6 Although its use was banned in the USA in 1972, residues of DDT could still be measured in human fat and breast milk ten years later.
7 Thomas R. Dunlap, *DDT: Scientists, Citizens, and Public Policy* (Princeton: Princeton University Press, 1981), p. 8.
8 *The New York Times*, national edn (July 1, 1982), p. 10.

9 Jim Mason and Peter Singer, *Animal Factories* (New York: Crown Publishers, 1980), p. 53. For the effects on the consumers, the farmers and the animals themselves of using factory methods to raise animals for human consumption, see also Peter Singer, *Animal Liberation: A New Ethics for Our Treatment of Animals* (New York: New York Review, 1975), ch. 3.

10 Donella H. Meadows, et al., *The Limits to Growth*, 2nd edn (New York: Universe Books, 1974), p. 147.

11 For a fuller discussion of the unanticipated consequences of the American aid to the Shah, see John L. Seitz, "The Failure of US Technical Assistance in Public Administration: The Iranian Case," *Public Administration Review*, 40 (September–October 1980), pp. 407–13.

12 E. F. Schumacher, *Small is Beautiful: Economics as if People Mattered* (New York: Harper and Row, 1973).

13 Emma Rothschild, *Paradise Lost: The Decline of the Auto-industrial Age* (New York: Random House, 1973), p. 119.

14 See, for example, Suzanne Arms, *Immaculate Deception: A New Look at Women and Childbirth in America* (New York: Bantam Books, 1977); Dr Robert A. Bradley, *Husband-coached Childbirth* (New York: Harper & Row, 1974); Gena Corea, "The Caesarean Epidemic," *Mother Jones* (July 1980); Barbara K. Rothman, "Midwives in Transition: The Structure of a Clinical Revolution," *Social Problems*, 30 (February 1983), pp. 262–71; Neal Devitt, "The Transition from Home to Hospital Birth in the United States, 1930–1960," *Birth and the Family Journal*, 4 (Summer 1977), pp. 47–58.

15 Dr John S. Miller, "Foreword," in Lester D. Hazell, *Commonsense Child-birth* (New York: Berkley Books, 1976), p. x.

16 Hardin, "The Tragedy of the Commons," p. 1243.

17 Jon R. Luoma, "The $33 Billion Misunderstanding," *Audubon*, 83 (November 1981), pp. 111–27.

18 This "missile gap," in which the Soviets trailed, could have been the reason they put missiles in Cuba in 1962, which led to the Cuban missile crisis, the world's first approach to the brink of nuclear war. The humiliation the USSR suffered when it had to take its missiles out of Cuba may have led to its recent large build-up of nuclear arms which has caused concern in the USA.

19 A train transporting a million tons of TNT would be 250 miles long.

20 Jonathan Schell, *The Fate of the Earth* (New York: Avon Books, 1982).

21 For a fuller description of the effects of a nuclear war see ibid., ch. 1; and Ruth Adams and Susan Cullen (eds), *The Final Epidemic:*

Physicians and Scientists on Nuclear War (Chicago: Bulletin of the Atomic Scientists, 1981). For a fuller discussion of the climatic changes – known as the "nuclear winter" thesis – which could occur after a nuclear war, see Carl Sagan, "Nuclear War and Climatic Catastrophe: Some Policy Implications," *Foreign Affairs*, 62 (Winter 1983/4), pp. 257–92; Thomas F. Malone, "International Scientists on Nuclear Winter," *Bulletin of the Atomic Scientists*, 41 (December 1985), pp. 52–5; and Starley Thompson and Stephen Schneider, "Nuclear Winter Reappraised," *Foreign Affairs*, 64 (Summer 1986), pp. 981–1005.

22 For an interesting discussion of the negative American attitude toward civil defense, see Freeman Dyson, *Weapons and Hope* (New York: Harper and Row), 1984, especially ch. 8.

23 Schell, *The Fate of the Earth*, p. 93.

7

Alternative Futures

In human affairs, the *logical* future, determined by past
and present conditions, is less important than the *willed*
future, which is largely brought about by deliberate
choices – made by the human free will.

René Dubos (1901–1982)

Where is development leading us? What can one say about the
future? Probably the wisest thing one can say is that the future is
essentially unknowable; it cannot be predicted. If this is so – and
the dismal record of past predictions leads one to believe it is – then
one might ask, "Does it make any sense to think about the future at
all?" I would answer, "Yes, it does." Although the complexity of
life and natural forces makes the future unknowable, human
actions can make one future more likely than another. It is this
ability to influence the future that concerns us in this final
chapter.

If we can accurately recognize some of the major trends and
currents in the past and the present, we can make an educated guess
about where we are heading. And if human beings do not like the
direction in which the world is heading, they can examine their
individual behavior and governmental policies to determine if they
should be changed so that they contribute to a more desired future.
René Dubos, the late well-known bacteriologist, helped coin the
phrase, "think globally, act locally." This is the way, according to
Dubos, that an individual can help bring about a desirable future.
One of the central themes of the book you are now finishing is that
politics – the process a society uses to achieve commonly desired
goals and to settle conflicts among groups with different interests –

will also play a central role in determining what the future will be like.

Of the many possible futures the human race faces on earth, three look most likely at present: doom, growth, and steady state. Some catastrophe might lead to the death of hundreds of millions of people; economic growth might continue into the future; or the world might achieve an equilibrium in its population growth, resource use, and production of goods. There could, of course, be a combination of two of these or of all three. For example, one part of the world might experience a harsher life in the future while another part continues to expand economically. Or part of the world could reach a steady state while another part continues to grow. In the rest of the chapter we will examine what the main proponents of these three views have to say, and end with my assessment of the future.

DOOM

There are a number of writings today warning that if humankind does not change its ways some kind of disaster will occur in the future. The implicit or explicit purpose of most of these authors is to help prevent the expected disaster by suggesting changes in human behavior or policies. Thus, these works are not really predictions of what the future will be like, but rather of what it could be like if present trends continue. The most frequently discussed disasters are those caused by nuclear war, food shortages, pollution, overpopulation, and the depletion of nonrenewable resources.

Nuclear War

Jonathan Schell in *The Fate of the Earth*[1] is probably the best-known writer at present who argues that the nation-state system, with its competition among big nations armed with nuclear weapons and with the proliferation of nuclear weapons to Third World nations, is leading the world to a nuclear war. Schell argues, as was pointed out more fully in chapter 6 on technology, that such a war could bring about the extinction of human life on our planet.

Pollution, Famines, Overpopulation, Resource Depletion

Since the early 1960s, several widely publicized books have been
written which forecast some sort of disaster coming because of
industrial pollution, scarcity of food, overpopulation, or depletion
of nonrenewable resources. One of the first was Rachel Carson's
Silent Spring, which predicted early death to humans and other
animals because of the growing use of pesticides and other
chemicals.[2] Another book which received about as much publicity
as Carson's was *The Population Bomb* by Paul Ehrlich. Ehrlich
spelled out the threat of overpopulation in the following terms:

> The battle to feed all of humanity is over. In the 1970s and
> 1980s hundreds of millions of people will starve to death in
> spite of any crash programs embarked upon now . . . no
> changes in behavior or technology can save us unless we can
> achieve control over the size of the human population. The
> birth rate must be brought into balance with the death rate or
> mankind will breed itself into oblivion.[3]

Another well known book was *The Limits to Growth*, which was a
report by the Club of Rome, a private group concerned with world
problems. The report was based on a computer analysis of the
world's condition by a research team at the Massachusetts Institute
of Technology. The book emphasized that the earth is finite and
that there are definite limits to its arable land, nonrenewable
resources, and ability to absorb pollution. The study's main
conclusion was as follows:

> If the present growth trends in world population, industrial-
> ization, pollution, food production, and resource depletion
> continue unchanged, the limits to growth on this planet will be
> reached sometime within the next one hundred years. The
> most probable result will be a rather sudden and uncontrollable
> decline in both population and industrial capacity.
>   It is possible to alter these growth trends and to establish a
> condition of ecological and economic stability that is sustainable
> far into the future.[4]

A second report of the Club of Rome in 1974, called *Mankind at the Turning Point*[5], forecast a similarly depressing future for the world if present trends continued; but, rather than predicting that a world collapse would occur, as *The Limits to Growth* study had done, it predicted that regional disasters and deteriorating conditions would lead to war.

In the late 1970s the US government conducted a three-year study of what the world would be like in the year 2000 if present trends continued. The conclusions of the *Global 2000 Report to the President* were consistent with those of the earlier Club of Rome studies:

If present trends continue, the world in 2000 will be more crowded, more polluted, less stable ecologically, and more vulnerable to disruption than the world we live in now. Serious stresses involving population, resources, and environment are clearly visible ahead. Despite greater material output, the world's people will be poorer in many ways than they are today.

For hundreds of millions of the desperately poor, the outlook for food and other necessities of life will be no better. For many it will be worse. Barring revolutionary advances in technology, life for most people on earth will be more precarious in 2000 than it is now – unless the nations of the world act decisively to alter current trends.[6]

The doomsday scenario is clearly seen in a major environmental textbook of the late 1970s, *Ecoscience*, by Paul Ehrlich, Anne Ehrlich, and John Holdren. The likelihood of approaching scarcities leading to war is a central feature of their conclusion:

[Our] brief survey of the dimensions of the human predicament suggests a discouraging outlook for the coming decades. A continuing set of interlocking shortages is likely – food, energy, raw materials – generating not only direct increases in human suffering and deprivation, but also increased political tension and (perversely) increased ability of the military wherewithal for LDCs [less developed countries] to relieve their frustrations aggressively. Resort to military action is possible, not only in the case of LDCs unwilling to suffer quietly, but, with equal or greater likelihood, in case of industrial powers whose high standard of living is threatened by denial of external resources.[7]

A forecast of doom for the future of mankind has led some authors to recommend policies designed to deal with such situations. One called "triage" was discussed in *Famine–1975!* by William and Paul Paddock.[8] Triage is a procedure which was used in World War I when doctors in battlefield hospitals had to decide which of the many wounded would receive the limited medical care available. The wounded were divided into three categories. The first were those soldiers who were only slightly wounded and, although in pain, would probably survive even if untreated. The second category consisted of soldiers who were so seriously wounded that even if they received medical attention, they would probably die. In the third category were soldiers who were seriously wounded but who could probably be saved if the doctors treated them. It was to the last category that the military doctors first turned their attention. The Paddock brothers recommended that the USA place the countries of the world who were requesting food aid into three categories similar to those in the triage procedure and give aid only to those countries in the third category, that is, to those which would have a good chance of progressing to a state of being able to survive by their own efforts if they received some aid.

"Lifeboat ethics" is a policy suggested by biologist Garrett Hardin in a world of desperately poor and overcrowded countries.[9] Hardin used the metaphor of lifeboats at sea, some of which are threatened to be swamped by people in the water trying to get in. According to Hardin, the people in the lifeboats, which are not completely filled, have three choices. The first is to take in everyone who wants to get on board; but that will lead to the lifeboat being swamped and everyone drowning. The second choice is to take on only a few to fill the empty seats; but that will lead to the loss of the small margin of safety and make for a very difficult decision as to which few will be selected. The third choice is to take no further people on board and to protect against boarding parties. Hardin saw the rich nations of the world as being in partially filled lifeboats and the poor nations as being in overcrowded boats with people spilling into the water because of their inability to control their population growth. Hardin recommends the third choice for the USA. He admits this is probably unjust, but recommends that those who feel guilty about it can trade places with those in the water. Good-willed but basically misguided efforts by the USA to aid poor countries, such as by giving them food during famines, can lead to more suffering in the long run. The emergency food aid contributes to a larger population eventually and thus a deeper crisis in the future.

GROWTH

Julian Simon, Professor of Business at the University of Maryland, is one of the main spokespersons for the second position on the future, that economic growth will and should continue indefinitely into the future. The following is a summary of the argument Simon presents in his book *The Ultimate Resource*.[10]

Natural resources are not finite in any real economic sense. When there is a temporary scarcity of a mineral, prices rise and the increased price stimulates new efforts to find more ore and more efficient methods to process it. The higher price also leads to the search for substitutes which are able to provide the same service as the temporarily scarce mineral. In fact, the cost of most minerals has actually been decreasing, so in a real sense minerals are becoming less scarce rather than more scarce. There are large deposits of minerals in the sea and even on the moon which have not yet been tapped. There is no need to conserve natural resources because of the needs of future generations or of poor nations. The present consumption of natural resources stimulates the production of them and improves the efficiency with which they are produced. Both of these developments will aid future generations. Poor nations are not helped by the rich nations using fewer resources; what the poor nations need is economic growth and that growth depends on their increased use of resources.

As with natural resources, the long-run future of energy looks very promising. Aside from temporary price increases caused by the political maneuvering of some countries, the long-run trend of the cost of energy has been downward. Over time, an hour's work has bought more rather than less electricity. This means that energy has become less scarce rather than more scarce. It is likely that an expanding population will speed the development of cheap energy supplies that are almost inexhaustible. In the past, increased demand for energy led to the discovery of new sources, new types of energy, and improved extraction processes. There is no reason why this trend should not continue into the future. Much of the world has not even been systemically explored for oil.

It is true that the more developed an economy becomes the more pollution it produces, but overall we live in a healthier environment than ever before. The best indicator of the level of pollution is length of life, indicated by the average life expectancy of the population. Life expectancy is rising, not falling, around the world. In the USA and other developed nations it has been rising for the past several centuries, and in the less developed nations for the past several decades. Although a rising income in a country often means more pollution, it also means a greater desire to clean up the pollution and an increased capacity to pay for cleaning it up. If one doesn't believe this, one can compare the cleanliness of streets in rich countries with those in poor countries.

Since World War II, the per capita food situation in the world has been improving. Famines have become fewer during the past century. The price of wheat has fallen over the long run. The trend toward cheaper grains should continue into the future. Overall, nutrition has been improving and there is no reason why it shouldn't continue to improve into the indefinite future. The amount of agricultural land on the planet has been increasing, especially as irrigation spreads. The amount of arable land is likely to continue to increase and it is not unrealistic to think about land becoming available on other planets. The colonizing of space is not an impossible dream any more.

Additional children mean costs to the society in the short run, but in the long run these children become producers, producing much more than they consume. For both less developed and more developed countries, a moderately growing population is likely to lead to a higher standard of living in the future than is a stationary, or rapidly increasing, population. When additional children are born both the mothers and the fathers work harder and spend less time in leisure. Also, a larger population means a bigger market which makes economies of scale possible; that is, industries can adopt more efficient procedures since they are producing more products for more buyers.

Past studies of animal behavior have often been cited as evidence that crowding is unhealthy, both psychologically and socially, for human beings. This is probably true for animals, but not for human beings. Isolation is what harms human beings, not crowding. In fact, a dense population makes necessary and economical an efficient transportation system. Such a system is essential for economic growth. A dense population also improves communications, something anyone can see by comparing a newspaper in a large city with one produced in a small city. A growing population spurs the adoption of existing technology and the search for new technology as well as the search for and production of new natural resources and energy.

The main question one should ask oneself when considering population is, What value do you place on human life? Who is to say that the life of a poor person is not of value? Who is to say that a country of 50 million people with a yearly per capita income of $4000 is better than a country with 100 million people and a per capita income of $3000? The most important resource we have on earth is the human mind. The human mind is the source of knowledge. The more human minds we have, the more knowledge we will have to solve the problems we face.

STEADY STATE

Lester Brown, head of the Worldwatch Institute, a research group established to analyze global problems, is considered one of the main spokespersons for the third position, that the world can and must achieve a sustainable or steady-state society in the future. Brown maintains that economic growth is undermining the carrying capacity of the earth to support life. His book, *Building a Sustainable Society*,[11] was published in 1981, the same year Julian Simon's book was published. The following is a summary of what a steady-state society would look like, according to Brown.

Population growth cannot continue indefinitely on a finite planet. Nations of the world should strive to achieve a relatively stable population of about 6 billion by the year 2020 instead of letting the world's population reach 10 billion, which the UN and the World Bank now project will be reached before the population stabilizes. With the right policies, there is no reason why the lower figure cannot be achieved. Even with 6 billion people the world will be hard pressed to maintain decent conditions for all. Human efforts must be focused on improving the human condition, and that requires a stable population.

In a steady-state society the population will not be concentrated in huge urban centers as it is now, but will be widely dispersed in relatively smaller communities which are near renewable energy sources. These communities, as well as individuals and nations, will achieve greater self-reliance; they will be less dependent on others for their prosperity than is the case today.

Renewable energy, whose ultimate source is the sun, will dominate in a steady-state society. The economic system will be redesigned to reduce the need for energy. Declining petroleum supplies will be conserved by carrying out present activities more efficiently and by curtailing some unnecessary activities. Better planning at the community and personal level will reduce the use of the automobile; more travel will be by rail and by bus.

There will be a resurgence in agriculture in the steady-state society as agriculture will be used to grow energy crops as well as to grow food and produce animal feed, and fiber. The trend in the Third World will be to manage the land more intensely by using more labor. Large landholdings, which are common now in the Third World, will be broken up.

A world-wide network of Biosphere Reserves will help protect species in their natural habitats. The UN Educational, Scientific, and Cultural Organization (UNESCO) has already decided to help establish such reserves.

National land use planning and erosion control will protect rich crop land in a steady state. Overgrazing and overfishing will be arrested and procedures established to maximize a sustainable yield. Large-scale tree planting will reverse deforestation and produce important economic and ecological benefits.

A throw-away society in the wealthy nations, which revolves around the planned obsolescence of products, will be replaced with one which emphasizes the durability of products and the recycling of used materials. This change will greatly reduce wastes, energy use, and inflation.

Globally, the funds spent for Research and Development are now dominated by military expenditures. This will probably need to change if a steady-state society is to be established. Vast sums of investment capital, both public and private, will be needed to finance the transition to a steady state – funds for energy-related projects, population stabilization programs, soil conservation, and reforestation.

Values which are dominant in a steady-state society will be significantly different from those which are common in the developed world today. A change from the present desire to dominate nature will be replaced with a desire to live in harmony with nature. This change will produce a new reverence for the land. The question of equity – that is, what is a fair distribution of wealth within and among societies – will receive new attention in a steady-state society. For the affluent, materialism – the search for happiness by continually acquiring new material goods – will be replaced with a new ethic of voluntary simplicity, which will limit the acquisition of goods only to satisfy basic needs. The focus of life will be placed on personal development, which includes improving human relations and achieving intellectual and spiritual growth.

CONCLUSIONS

Could the world's future contain parts of all three alternative futures presented in this chapter? I believe it could. The dangers that the "doom" alternative conveys are real. Some of them have already taken place in parts of the earth, such as overpopulation in India and China, famine in Africa, and toxic poisoning in the USA. The threat of nuclear war is widely recognized. If actions are not taken to reduce the nuclear threat, to reduce the population growth in the poorer nations, and to end some forms of environmental deterioration, it is possible that huge loss of life could occur in the future. The positive feature of the doom scenario is that it causes us to recognize real dangers and to try to prevent them from occurring. The negative aspect of this imagined future is that for some people it can weaken their will to act. It frightens them so much that they literally give up on the future, becoming either depressed, numb, or inclined to live for the present. Too much preaching of doom can be a self-fulfilling prophecy if its effect is to discourage action.

The "growth" future appears to be a good one for the developing nations to strive for. They need more economic growth in order to raise their living standards. To attempt to achieve a more equal distribution of income in many of these countries today without further growth would create tremendous political turmoil and would probably bring little benefit to their societies, since in many of these countries there isn't that much economic wealth to redistribute. To argue that these countries should not grow economically would be to condemn them to living forever with their present poverty. But to advocate more economic growth for the less developed nations does not deny the need for many of these nations to achieve a more equal distribution of income. The growth-with-equity approach presented in chapter 1 holds out the possibility that both growth and equity can be achieved in the Third World. And to advocate more economic growth for the less developed nations does not deny their vital need to slow down their population growth and to move toward a stable population.

But does more economic growth make sense in the developed nations? It is unpopular today to suggest that it does not, but this may indeed be the case. The desire in the wealthy nations to acquire more and more material possessions has placed a tremendous strain on the planet. This book has been concerned with documenting that strain. The developed nations have achieved for most of their citizens the goal that only kings and queens could achieve in the past – material comfort, an abundance of food, a relatively long life, and leisure. But these countries are finding it very difficult to learn when enough is enough. Obsession with materialism has been condemned by many of the great religions of the world, but it is still an obsession experienced by many. It is not hard to recognize that this obsession is not healthy – for the individual or for the planet – and that human beings need a different goal for their lives. Aleksandr Solzhenitsyn, the great twentieth century Russian writer, believes that this goal should be "the quest for worthy spiritual growth" rather than the pursuit of material success.[12]

The steady-state future appears to be the one the developed

nations should strive for, since we live in a world in which some of the resources needed to support life are finite. A steady-state world would not mean the absence of growth, but the growth which would be emphasized would be intellectual, moral, and spiritual rather than the growth of material objects. It would not mean the end to the striving to find better ways of doing things, or the end to the search for new solutions to human problems. Human beings need challenges; a steady-state society should contain them.

Although there is little prospect at present of the developed nations adopting the steady state as their goal, or even an interest in the possibility, it may come. The USA is already moving toward an economy in which occupations which utilize new knowledge will soon be more common than blue-collar manufacturing jobs.[13] And nearly all industrialized nations have already achieved a birth rate which is at or below replacement level, thus leading to a relatively stable population for them in the not too distant future.

And there is a slowly growing awareness in the developed nations – as well as in parts of the Third World – that human beings need to live in harmony with nature, to move beyond their compulsion to dominate it. For people who don't yet have this awareness, one of the best ways they can learn this is by personal experience. When they learn, for example, that the water they have been drinking contains cancer-producing chemicals, they learn a lesson about ecology better than any textbook could teach them. Human beings can also learn by using their reason; their use of this capacity can make personal experience less needed as a teaching tool. But either way, human beings can and do learn and change their ways when their own survival depends on it.

We do not know if life exists elsewhere in the universe. It may, on some planets around the billions of stars in our galaxy or in the billions of other galaxies. But as far as we know, we are the only life that exists. In such a situation, to preserve life on this planet and to improve the human condition must be the goal of development. No other will do.

NOTES

1 Jonathan Schell, *The Fate of the Earth* (New York: Avon Books, 1982).

2 Rachel Carson, *Silent Spring* (Greenich, Conn.: Fawcett Books, 1962.

3 Paul R. Ehrlich, *The Population Bomb*, revised edn (New York: Ballantine Books, 1971), pp. xi–xii.

4 Donella Meadows et al., *The Limits to Growth*, 2nd edn (New York: Universe Books, 1974), p. 24.

5 Mihajlo Mesarovic and Eduard Pestel, *Mankind at the Turning Point* (New York: New American Library, 1974).

6 Council on Environmental Quality and the Department of State, *The Global 2000 Report to the President*, vol. 1 (New York: Penguin Books, 1982), p. 1.

7 Paul R. Ehrlich, Anne H. Ehrlich, and John P. Holdren, *Ecoscience: Population, Resources, Environment*, (San Francisco: W. H. Freeman, 1977), p. 5.

8 William Paddock and Paul Paddock, *Famine–1975!* (Boston: Little, Brown, 1967), ch. 9.

9 Garrett Hardin, "Living on a Lifeboat," *Bioscience*, 24 (October 1974), pp. 561–8.

10 Julian Simon, *The Ultimate Resource* (Princeton: Princeton University Press, 1981).

11 Lester Brown, *Building a Sustainable Society* (New York: W. W. Norton, 1981).

12 Aleksandr Solzhenitsyn, "Men Have Forgotten God," *National Review* (July 22, 1983), p. 876.

13 *New York Times*, nat. edn (August 15, 1986), p. 26. For a discussion of some of these trends, see also John Naisbitt, *Megatrends: Ten New Directions Transforming Our Lives* (New York: Warner Books, 1982).

Selected Bibliography

Adams, Ruth and Susan Cullen (eds), *The Final Epidemic: Physicians and Scientists on Nuclear War* (Chicago: Bulletin of the Atomic Scientists, 1981).

Adelman, Irma and Cynthia Taft Morris, *Economic Growth and Social Equity in Developing Countries* (Stanford, Cal.: Stanford University Press, 1973).

Albright, David, "Chernobyl and the US Nuclear Industry," *Bulletin of the Atomic Scientists*, 42 (November 1986), pp. 38–40.

Arms, Suzanne, *Immaculate Deception: A New Look at Women and Childbirth in America* (New York: Bantam Books, 1977).

Barnet, Richard, *The Lean Years: Politics in the Age of Scarcity* (New York: Simon and Schuster, 1980).

Berger, Peter, "Underdevelopment Revisited," *Commentary*, 78 (July 1984), pp. 41–5.

Bernstein, Jeremy, "Recreating the Power of the Sun," *New York Times Magazine* (January 3, 1982), pp. 14–53.

Brown, Lester R., *The Twenty-ninth Day* (New York: W. W. Norton, 1978).

——, *Building a Sustainable Society* (New York: W. W. Norton, 1981).

——, and Edward Wolf, "Food Crisis in Africa," *Natural History*, 93 (June 1984), pp. 16–20.

——, et al., *State of the World* (New York: W. W. Norton, annual).

Brown, Michael, *Laying Waste: The Poisoning of America by Toxic Wastes* (New York: Pantheon Books, 1980).

Calder, Nigel, *Nuclear Nightmares: An Investigation Into Possible Wars* (New York: Penguin Books, 1979).

Carson, Rachel, *Silent Spring* (Greenwich, Conn.: Fawcett Books, 1962).

Commoner, Barry, *The Closing Circle* (New York: Alfred Knopf, 1971).

——, *The Politics of Energy* (New York: Alfred Knopf, 1979).

Council on Environmental Quality, *Global Energy Futures and the Carbon*

Dioxide Problem (Washington, DC: Council on Environmental Quality, 1981).

——, and the Department of State, *The Global 2000 Report to the President: Entering the Twenty-first Century*, vol. 1 (Washington, DC: US Government Printing Office, 1980; New York: Penguin, 1982).

——, *Global Future: Time to Act* (Washington, DC: US Government Printing Office, 1981).

Critchfield, Richard, *Villages* (Garden City, NY: Anchor Press/Doubleday, 1981).

——, "Science and the Villager: The Last Sleeper Wakes," *Foreign Affairs*, 61 (Fall 1982), pp. 14–41.

Darmstadter, Joel, "Economic Growth and Energy Conservation: Historical and International Lessons," Reprint no. 154 (Washington, DC: Resources for the Future, 1978).

Deese, David A. and Joseph S. Nye (eds), *Energy and Security* (Cambridge, Mass.: Ballinger, 1981).

Deudney, Daniel and Christopher Flavin, *Renewable Energy* (New York: W. W. Norton, 1983).

DeWalt, Billie, "The Cattle Are Eating the Forest," *Bulletin of the Atomic Scientists*, 39 (January 1983), pp. 18–23.

Dubos, René, "A Celebration of Life," *First-Class, World Wide*, 1 (April 1982), pp. 9 and 102.

Dunlap, Thomas R., *DDT: Scientists, Citizens, and Public Policy* (Princeton, NJ: Princeton University Press, 1981).

Durant, Mary, "Here We Go A-Bottling" [recycling], *Audubon*, 88 (May 1986), pp. 32–5.

Dyson, Freeman, *Weapons and Hope* (New York: Harper and Row, 1984).

Eckholm, Erik P. *Down to Earth: Environment and Human Needs* (New York: W. W. Norton, 1982).

Egginton, Joyce, "The Long Island Lesson" [polluting the ground water], *Audubon*, 83 (July 1981), pp. 84–93.

——, "Just a Farm Story" [toxic waste incinerators and agriculture], *Audubon*, 87 (November 1985), pp. 134–43.

Ehrlich, Paul R. and Anne H. Ehrlich, *Extinction* (New York: Random House, 1981).

——, and John P. Holdren, *Ecoscience: Population, Resources, Environment* (San Francisco: W. H. Freeman, 1977).

Eicher, Carl, "Facing Up to Africa's Food Crisis," *Foreign Affairs*, 61 (Fall 1982), pp. 151–74.

Farvar, M. Taghi and John Milton (eds), *The Careless Technology: Ecology and International Development* (Garden City, NY: Natural History Press, 1972).

Freed, Stanley and Ruth Freed, "One Son Is No Sons," *Natural History*, 94 (January 1985), pp. 10–15.

Freeman, Christopher and Marie Jahoda (eds), *World Futures: The Great Debate* (New York: Universe Books, 1978).

Green, Harold, "The Peculiar Politics of Nuclear Power," *The Bulletin of the Atomic Scientists*, 38 (December 1982), pp. 59–65.

Guppy, Nicholas, "Tropical Deforestation: A Global View," *Foreign Affairs*, 62 (Spring 1984), pp. 928–65.

Halle, Louis, "A Hopeful Future for Mankind," *Foreign Affairs*, 58 (Summer 1980), pp. 1129–36.

Hardin, Garrett, "The Tragedy of the Commons," *Science*, 162 (December 13, 1968), pp. 1243–8.

——, "Living on a Lifeboat," *Bioscience*, 24 (October 1974), pp. 561–8.

Holdren, John P., "Nuclear Power and Nuclear Weapons: The Connection is Dangerous," *Bulletin of the Atomic Scientists*, 39 (January 1983), pp. 40–5.

Hopkins, Raymond, Robert Paarlberg, and Mitchel Wallerstein, *Food in the Global Arena: Actors, Values, Policies and Futures* (New York: Holt, Rinehart and Winston, 1982).

Insel, Barbara, "A World Awash in Grain," *Foreign Affairs*, 63 (Spring 1985), pp. 892–911.

Jackson, Henry, "The African Crisis: Drought and Debt," *Foreign Affairs*, 63 (Summer 1985), pp. 1081–94.

Kellogg, William and Robert Schware, "Society, Science and Climate Change," *Foreign Affairs*, 60 (Summer 1982), pp. 1076–1109.

Kramer, Mark, *Three Farms: Making Milk, Meat and Money from the American Soil* (Boston: Little, Brown, 1980).

LaBastille, Anne, "Heaven, Not Hell" [development in the Amazon Basin], *Audubon*, 81 (November 1979), pp. 68–103.

Lappé, Frances Moore and Joseph Collins, *Food First: Beyond the Myth of Scarcity* (New York: Ballantine Books, 1978).

Levine, Adeline, *Love Canal: Science, Politics and People* (Lexington, Mass.: Lexington Books, 1982).

Lewis, W. Arthur, "The State of Development Theory," *The American Economic Review*, 74 (March 1984), pp. 1–9.

Lovins, Amory, L. Hunter Lovins, and Leonard Ross, "Nuclear Power and Nuclear Bombs," *Foreign Affairs* (Summer 1980), pp. 1137–77.

Luoma, Jon, "Troubled Skies, Troubled Waters" [acid rain], *Audubon*, 82 (November 1980), pp. 88–111.

——, "Forests are Dying But Is Acid Rain Really to Blame," *Audubon*, 89 (March 1987), pp. 37–51.

——, "The $33 Billion Misunderstanding" [sewage plants and clean water], *Audubon*, 83 (November 1981), pp. 110–27.

Mahler, Halfdan, "People," *Scientific American*, 243 (September 1980), pp. 67–77.

Marden, Parker, G., Dennis G. Hodgson, and Terry L. McCoy, *Population in the Global Arena: Actors Values, Policies, and Futures* (New York: Holt, Rinehart and Winston, 1982).

Mason, Jim and Peter Singer, *Animal Factories* (New York: Crown Publishers, 1980).

McNamara, Robert, "Time Bomb or Myth: The Population Problem," *Foreign Affairs*, 62 (Summer 1984), pp. 1107–31.

Meadows, Donella H., et al., *The Limits to Growth*, 2nd edn (New York: Universe Books, 1974).

Merrick, Thomas, W., "World Population in Transition," *Population Bulletin*, 41 (April 1986), pp. 1–51.

Miller, Lynn, *Global Order: Values and Power in International Politics* (Boulder, Colorado: Westview Press, 1985).

Murphy, Elaine, *World Population: Toward the Next Century*, revised edn (Washington, DC: Population Reference Bureau, 1985).

Myers, Norman, "The Exhausted Earth," *Foreign Policy*, 42 (Spring 1981), pp. 141–55.

——, "Room in the Ark?" *Bulletin of the Atomic Scientists*, 38 (November 1982), pp. 44–8.

——, *The Primary Source* (New York: W. W. Norton, 1984).

National Audubon Society, *The Audubon Energy Plan* (New York: National Audubon Society, 1984).

National Research Council, *Energy in Transition 1985–2010* (San Francisco: W H. Freeman, 1980).

——, *Population Growth and Economic Development: Policy Questions* (Washington, DC: National Academy Press, 1986).

Nelkin, Dorothy, "Some Social and Political Dimensions of Nuclear Power: Examples from Three Mile Island," *American Political Science Review*, 75 (March 1981), pp. 132–42.

Ophuls, William, *Ecology and the Politics of Scarcity* (San Francisco: W. H. Freeman, 1977).

Peterson, Jeannie (ed.), "Nuclear War: The Aftermath," *Ambio*, 11, no. 2–3, (1982), pp. 76–176.

Pirages, Dennis, *The New Context for International Relations: Global Ecopolitics* (North Scituate, Mass.: Duxbury Press, 1978).

Population Reference Bureau, *World Population Data Sheet* (Washington, DC: Population Reference Bureau, annual).

Portney, Paul (ed.), *Current Issues in Natural Resource Policy* (Washington, DC: Resources for the Future, 1982).

Presidential Commission on World Hunger, *Overcoming World Hunger: The Challenge Ahead* (Washington, DC: US Government Printing Office, 1980).

Prosterman, Roy L. *The Decline in Hunger-related Deaths*, The Hunger Project Papers, no. 1 (San Francisco: The Hunger Project, 1984).

Rasmussen, Wayne and Paul Stone, "Toward a Third Agricultural Revolution," *Food Policy and Farm Programs: Proceedings of the Academy of Political Science*, 34, no. 3 (1982), pp. 174–85.

Raven, Peter, "Tropical Rain Forests: A Global Responsibility," *Natural History*, 90 (February 1981), pp. 28–32.

Royston, Michael, "Making Pollution Prevention Pay," *Harvard Business Review* (November–December 1980), pp. 6–14.

Sagan, Carl, "Nuclear War and Climatic Catastrophe: Some Policy Implications," *Foreign Affairs*, 62 (Winter 1983/4), pp. 257–92.

Sampson, R. Neil, "Soil Conservation," *Sierra* (November–December 1983), pp. 40–4.

Sant, Roger, Steven C. Carhard et al., *Eight Great Energy Myths: The Least-cost Energy Strategy – 1978–2000* (Arlington, Va.: Energy Productivity Center of the Mellon Institute, 1981).

Sassin, Wolfgang, "Energy," *Scientific American*, 243 (September 1980), pp. 119–32.

Schell, Jonathan, *The Fate of the Earth* (New York: Avon Books, 1982).

Schumacher, E. F., *Small is Beautiful: Economics as if People Mattered* (New York: Harper and Row, 1973).

Scrimshaw, Nevin and Lance Taylor, "Food," *Scientific American*, 243 (September 1980), pp. 78–88.

Short, R. V., "Breast Feeding," *Scientific American*, 250 (April 1984), pp. 35–41.

Simon, Julian, *The Ultimate Resource* (Princeton, NJ: Princeton University Press, 1981).

——, and Herman Kahn (eds), *The Resourceful Earth* (Oxford, England: Basil Blackwell, 1984).

Singer, Peter, *Animal Liberation: A New Ethics for Our Treatment of Animals* (New York: New York Review, 1975).

Sivard, Ruth, *World Military and Social Expenditures* (Washington, DC: World Priorities, annual).

Skolnick, Jerome and Elliott Currie, *Crisis in American Institutions*, 6th edn (Boston: Little, Brown, 1985).

Smil, Vaclav, "Ecological Mismanagement in China," *Bulletin of the Atomic Scientists*, 38 (October 1982), pp. 18–23.

Solar Energy Research Institute, *A New Prosperity: Building a Sustainable Energy Future* (Andover, Mass.: Brick House Publishing, 1981.

Solomon, Stephen, "The Controversy Over Infant Formula," *New York Times Magazine* (December 6, 1981), pp. 92–106.

Spinrad, Bernard, "Nuclear Power and Nuclear Weapons: The Connection is Tenuous," *Bulletin of the Atomic Scientists*, 39 (February 1983), pp. 42–7.

Sprout, Harold and Margaret Sprout, *The Context of Environmental Politics* (Lexington, Ky: University Press of Kentucky, 1978).

Starr, Roger, "The Case for Nuclear Energy," *New York Times Magazine* (November 8, 1981), pp. 122–9.

Steinhart, Peter, "The Second Green Revolution," *New York Times Magazine* (October 25, 1981), pp. 46–64.

——, "Down in the Dumps" [solid wastes], *Audubon*, 88 (May 1986), pp. 104–9.

Stobaugh, Robert, and Daniel Yergin (eds), *Energy Future: Report of the Energy Project at the Harvard Business School* (New York: Ballantine Books, 1980).

Talbot, Ross, "Food in the American Political Economy," *Food Policy and Farm Programs: Proceedings of the Academy of Political Science*, 34 (1982), pp. 1–11.

Tarrant, John R., *Food Policies* (New York: John Wiley, 1980).

Thompson, Starley and Stephen Schneider, "Nuclear Winter Reappraised," *Foreign Affairs*, 64 (Summer 1986), pp. 981–1005.

Thurow, Lester, *The Zero-sum Society: Distribution and Possibilities for Economic Change* (New York: Basic Books, 1980).

Uhl, Christopher, "You Can Keep a Good Forest Down," *Natural History*, 92 (April 1983), pp. 71–9.

Ward, Barbara, *Progress for a Small Planet* (New York: W. W. Norton, 1979).

Weaver, James and Kenneth Jameson, *Economic Development: Competing Paradigms* (Washington, DC: University Press of America, 1981).

Weir, David and Mark Schapiro, *Circle of Poison* (San Francisco: Institute for Food and Development Policy, 1981).

Wolterding, Martin, "The Poisoning of Central America," *Sierra* (September–October 1981), pp. 63–7.

World Bank, *World Development Report* (New York: Oxford University Press, annual).

World Resources Institute, *Journal* (Washington, DC: World Resources Institute, annual).

—— and International Institute for Environment and Development, *World Resources* (New York: Basic Books, annual).

Yergin, Daniel and Martin Hillenbrand (eds), *Global Insecurity: A Strategy for Energy and Economic Renewal* (Boston: Houghton Mifflin, 1982).

Index